The Meaning of the "Numbers" of the Antichrist

BY

DAVID BERRY WATERFILL, M.D.

DORRANCE PUBLISHING CO., INC.
PITTSBURGH, PENNSYLVANIA 15222

All Rights Reserved
Copyright © 2002 by David Berry Waterfill, M.D.
No part of this book may be reproduced or transmitted
in any form or by any means, electronic or mechanical,
including photocopying, recording, or by any information
storage and retrieval system without permission in
writing from the publisher.

ISBN # 8-8059-5793-6
Printed in the United States of America

First Printing

For information or to order additional books, please write:
Dorrance Publishing Co., Inc.
643 Smithfield Street
Pittsburgh, Pennsylvania 15222
U.S.A.
1-800-788-7654
Or visit our web site and on-line catalog at *www.dorrancepublishing.com*

Table of Contents

Chapter 1: Near East Civilization 1

Chapter 2: Expansion of Civilization 19

Chapter 3: Medieval Ages
to Twenty First Century 40

Chapter 4: The Number of the Antichrist 41

Chapter 5: The Canaanite 43

Appendix 46

Bibliography 48

"Wisdom crieth aloud in the street…"
Prov. 1:20 Revised Version 1881–1885

Chapter One
Near East Civilization

The word "prehistory" denotes the study of human communities before writing was invented. In the past, archeologists spoke in phrases such as "palaeolithic savagery." I guess we're called "hunters and gatherers" nowadays. "Neolithic barbarism" described dependence on the two branches of agriculture, animal husbandry and horticulture.

Advancements during the prehistoric era included metallurgy, weaving, pottery making, and masonry with stone and brick. Copper was the first metal smelted for tools and weapons. It was next observed that adding tin to molten copper produced an alloy that was stronger than copper, which was known as bronze. These discoveries were first perfected in the Fertile Crescent and in the valley of the Nile River. Yet people all over the world had created mysterious drawings, erected megaliths, carved little amulets, and shown care in the burying of their dead for tens of thousands of years prior to the end of the Neolithic Age. Mud brick dwellings excavated at the bottom layers of habitation in the Near East date back at least to 4300 B.C. [1]

On the eastern side of the Fertile Crescent sits a region once known as Susiana or Elam. It was a country of foothills and mountain rivers that emptied into a productive plane near the Persian Gulf. Its central city was Susa, or Shushan. The land of Mesopotamia extended between the Tigris and Euphrates Rivers to the west of Elam. The southern end contained primeval swamps teeming with fish and game, and it had a hot climate. Writers of the Bible called it *Shinar*, which meant "country of two rivers." *Kengi(r)*, or "civilized land," was the name applied by the Sumerians. Babylonians named it *Sumer*.

The northern portion of Mesopotamia became the homelands of Akkad and Assyria. Westward, the Fertile Crescent incorporated Syria and the Levant. Around the outside of the crescent were mountains with foothills and valleys of grassland and forest. Toward the inside sat the desert.

The Nile River Valley is sometimes included as part of the Fertile Crescent. It was formed beside the Nile River by strips of land as much as thirty-three miles wide. These strips of land came to be inhabited during the Neolithic days. Originally, a great swampy forest grew there. The habitable sections were secluded behind harsh deserts on either side. Ten mighty cataracts interrupted the river's flow through its lengthy progression.

Elam was the place where, in much later times, the Babylonian and Persian kings built luxuriant palaces [2]. Its language was unrelated to any known ancient or modern tongue, and it has been only partially deciphered. The Elamites' form of government also was unique, being different even from those of nearby Sumerian cities.

Before we can grasp Elam's significance, we must think about life in the Neolithic, barbaric community. There was little personal property, other than individual dwellings, and not a lot of independent action. Decisions were made by a group of elders. Loyalty was to one's village and tribal relationships. Trade could be useful, but self-reliance was the rule. In the course of events somewhere, a group moved ahead of others both within and beyond their own borders. Many who were left behind were made to see themselves as being inadequate, even guilty. A few began striving too hard to try to catch up. Some within the more advanced society were at first full of guilt, but they usually justified their behaviors in a number of ways. They told themselves that their motivation was acceptable, and they invited selected outsiders to join them.

They became convinced that the outsiders had posed a threat from the beginning, and they shut themselves off further. In the end, they became accusatory and aggressive. Before long, anyone who remained involved was taken into spiritual captivity. As time went on, new generations and different people who came into power knew of no other way to live. Tyrannical warrior chieftains, and their shaman priests, elevated themselves into positions of power [3].

Social scientists have described a variety of family patterns found around the world. One is called the cognatic family. Under this family structure, the family name is passed down through the father, but there exists no prohibition against maintaining relationships with members on either the maternal or paternal side of one's family.

Somewhere along the line, some genius started appointing *names* to all the young men in his tribal territory. Rather suddenly, each individual, not just shamans and warrior chiefs, found within a gift of dignity and self worth. With one stroke of inspiration, a whole new set of loyalties came into existence. Thus, a liberating individualism was ordained, without unraveling needful order in communities [4].

Ancient Elam had a federated government structure. There was an overlord, who functioned as head of the government. He lived in the city of Susa. His next oldest brother was viceroy. The viceroy was the *heir presumptive*, which means that he was appointed overlord when his older brother died. The seat of his office was the ruling family's hometown. A regent, who shared power with the two figures referenced above, ruled the capital city of Susa itself. He was the overlord's son, or, if there were no competent son, the most capable and acceptable nephew. By such means, opportunity was opened for the next generation. The Elamites entered history, with written records, near the time of Mesopotamia. Their traditions derived from social developments and political decisions of the prehistoric era [5].

Prehistoric Elam maintained relations with four regions of the world. Surrounded by water on three sides, and with a desert plateau interspersed by oases in the middle, the Arabian peninsula lay to the southwest. Habitable areas were situated around the periphery, with the highest rainfall in the south. Settlements that traded with the Sumerians have been unearthed in modern Bahrain. Yet, watery pathways, which, from the perspective of Elam, "surrounded" or "bordered" the peninsula started in the Red Sea and ended somewhere in the Pacific Ocean.

Today, Indonesia has more Muslims than any other nation in the world. Its people were converted by Arab traders.

"Surrounding" or "bordering" the land of Cush were the Levant, the Sinai Peninsula, Egypt (with its river), and North Africa. An important migration of people from the shores of the western Mediterranean traversed this region during the late prehistoric era. They

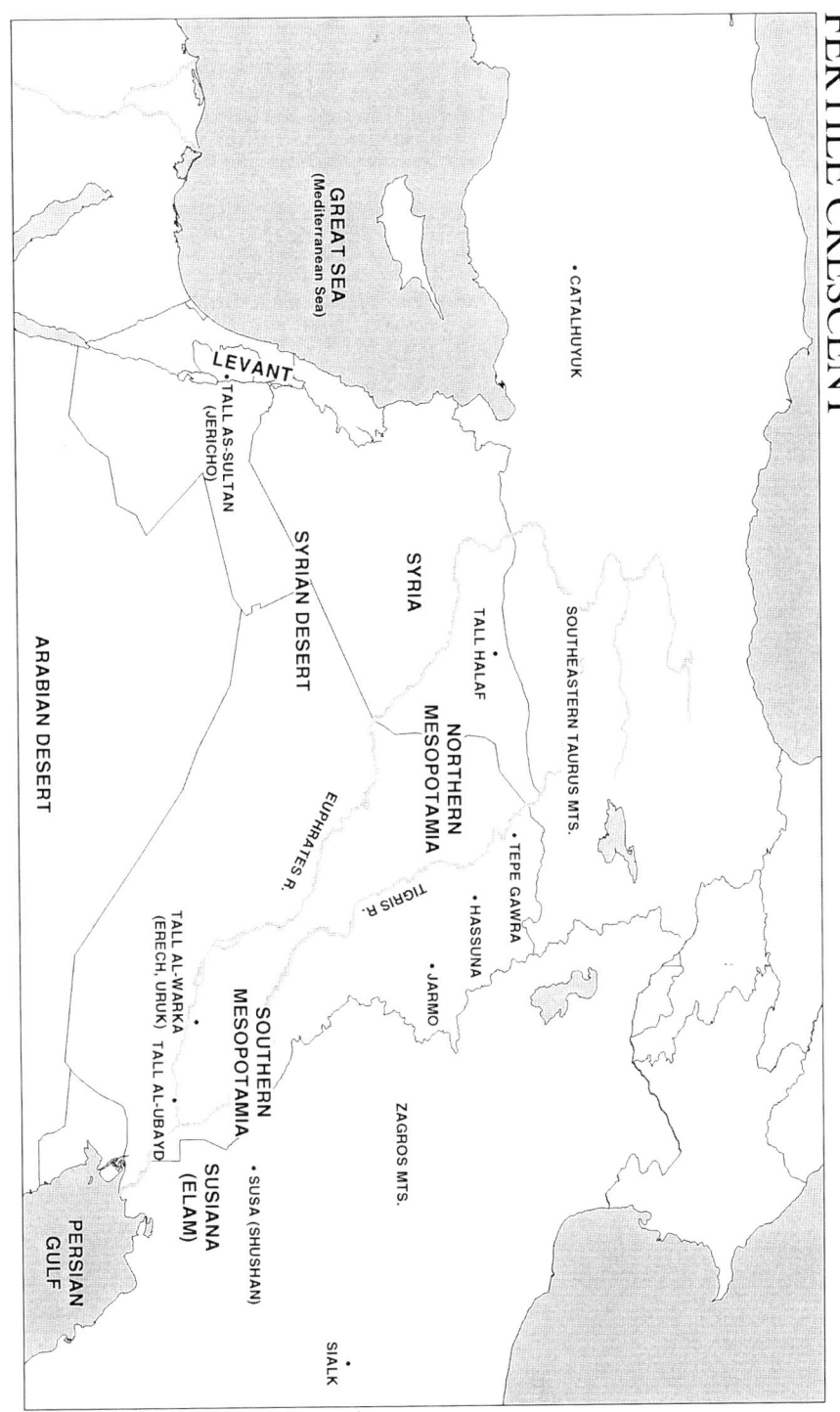

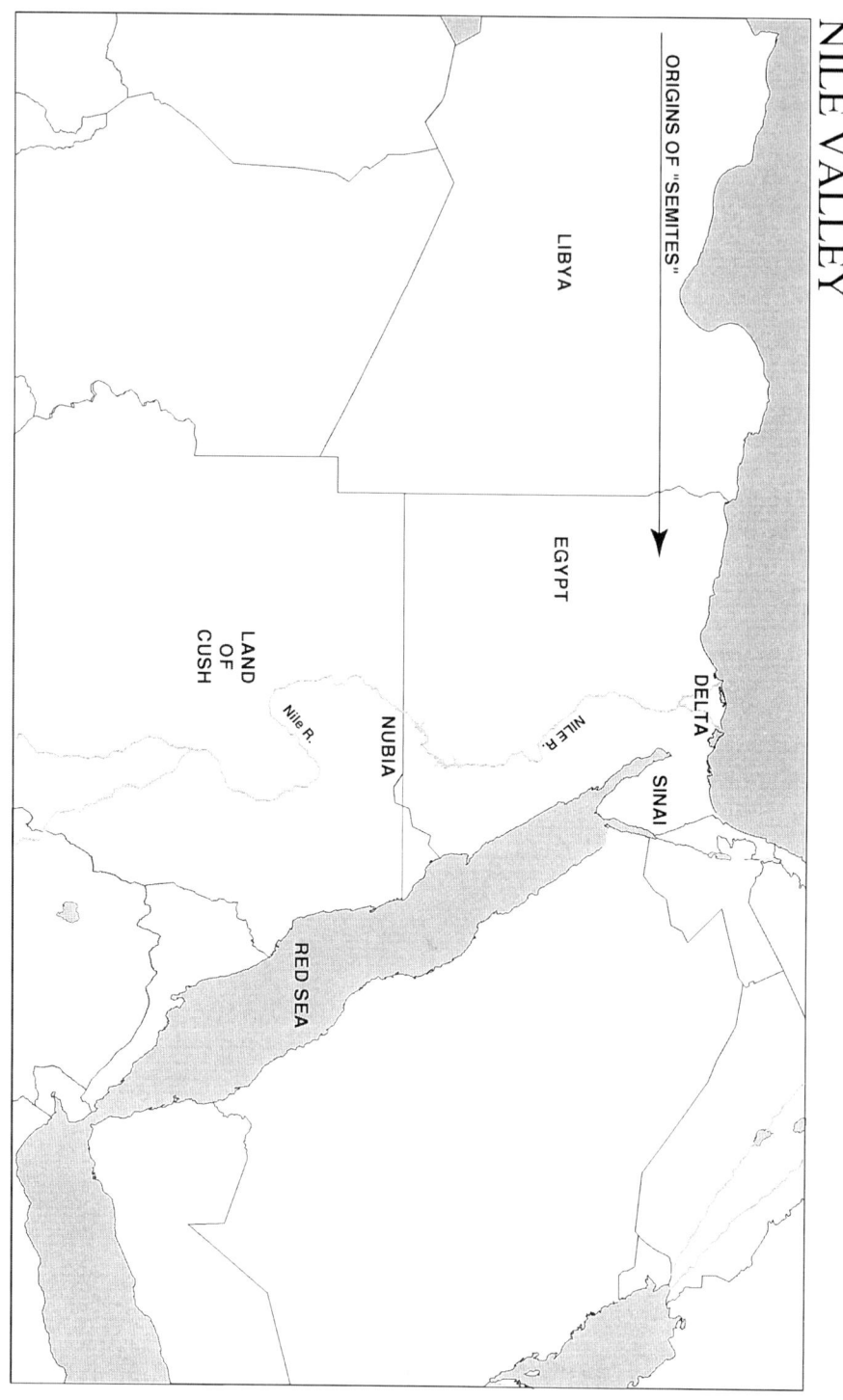

reached western Asia by at least 3000 B.C. In modern times, they continue to be known as Semites.

What is called Central Asia is a grassland that extends from eastern Europe to western China. To its north grew vast primeval forests. Deserts were to the south. It was in this region that the horse was first domesticated.

All across Europe, from the mouth of the Danube River to the British Isles, Neolithic villages had been sprouting up for a long time.

In *Old Testament* Hebrew, *Pishon* means "dispersive," and *Havilah*, "circular." *Bdellium* is a fragrant resin from a tree that grew in Arabia, Babylonia, Media, and India. The *onyx* corresponds scripturally to the old Hebrew tribal division of Joseph. The word *Gihon* means "gushing." Whereas the exact meaning of *Hiddekel* (Tigris) remains uncertain to this day, *Euphrates* still stands for "rushing [6]." "*Chay*," in Hebrew, has been defined as "alive." This word was written at least twenty-eight times in the book of *Genesis*, chapters one through nine. Sometimes, the word *living* is used in English language Bibles to define the word "*Chay*." In other instances, translators considered the word *beast* more appropriate [7].

River Hiddekel and River Euphrates, as a general rule, reach northward. Pishon and Gihon flow, generally, toward the south. And what about the garden of Eden before its inhabitants gave ear to the vengeful fantasies of a big-talking loser? The word meant "pleasure. [8]"

The deeper levels of habitation uncovered at Susa contained pottery of finer quality than that from more shallow, later layers [9]. Elam's early development occurred in conjunction with that of Shinar [10].

Permanent human habitation had long been established in southern Mesopotamia when Sumerians came in from the East, which was completed, at the latest, by 3300 B.C. The region had never provided many natural resources: water, food, and clay to make into pottery and brick were the only locally available materials. Trade had been necessary to maintain the economy. A beautiful blue stone, lapis lazuli, was brought from as far as the Oxus River in the East. Amber filtered in via connections to the Jutland Peninsula in northern Europe. A variety of items could be obtained from Asia Minor, Syria, modern Oman, the valley of the Indus River, and even India. Eventually, tin was imported by intermediaries out of Phoenicia, Kittim, the Aegean, and Tarshish from as far as the Iberian Peninsula and Cornwall in southern Britain! The world's first *high civilization* came into being following the Sumerians' arrival [11].

Various characteristics must come together to generate societies with such a degree of complexity. One is economic specialization. In the barbaric village, the only distinction of activity was between the sexes. Every man pretty much knew how to do every masculine job, each woman every feminine job. The men focused on domesticating animals, the women on growing gardens. After the arrival of civilization, men took over, and women vacated, horticulture. All forms of agriculture had to be standardized to produce the extra food required by those not involved directly in its production. Pottery and brick making became industries. Metallurgists organized secret societies. Metal was not always plentiful, and their know-how was indispensable to warrior chiefs for weapons manufacturing. Shamans, gathering in sacred colleges, sanctified themselves as full-time

The Meaning of the Numbers of the Antichrist

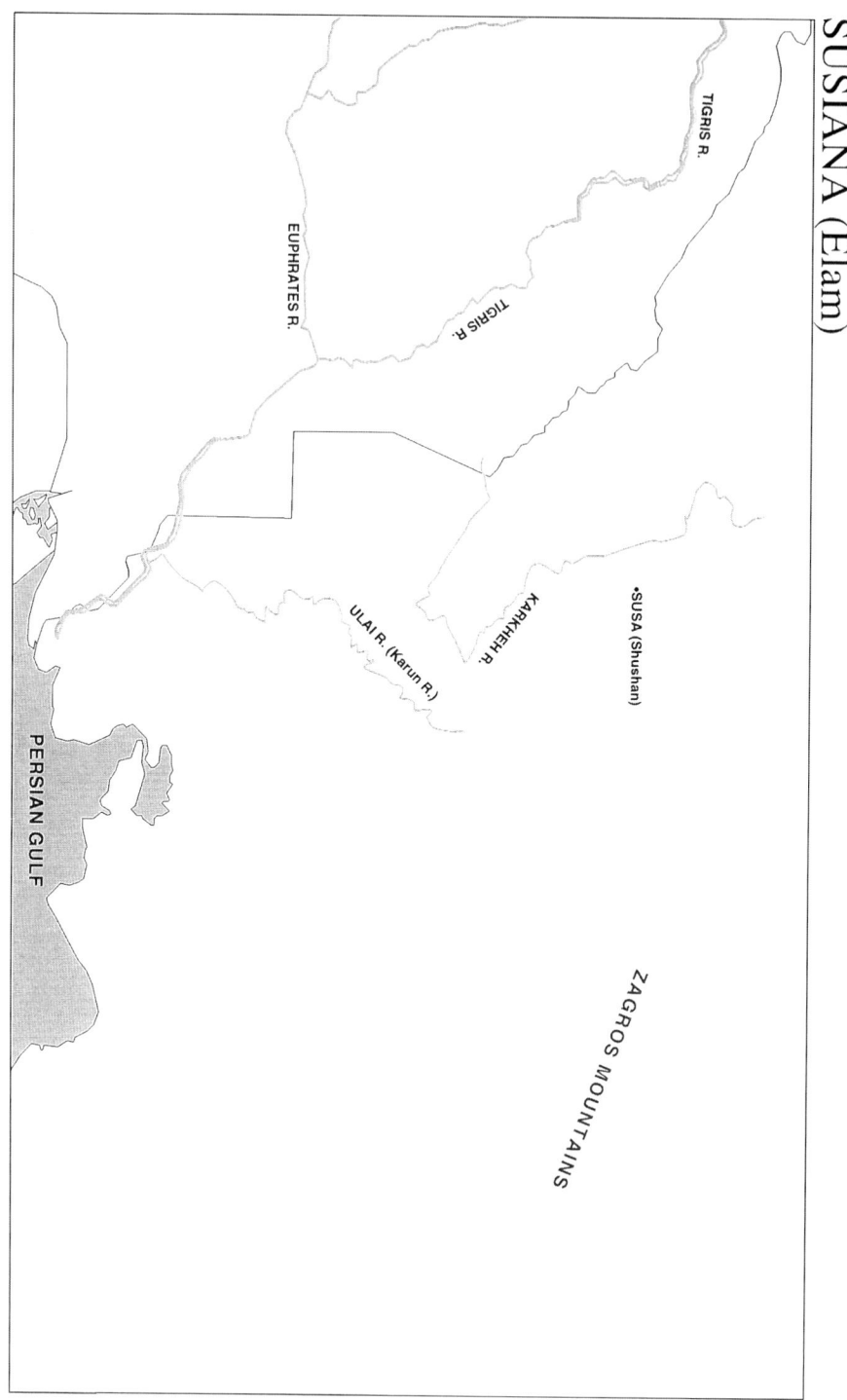

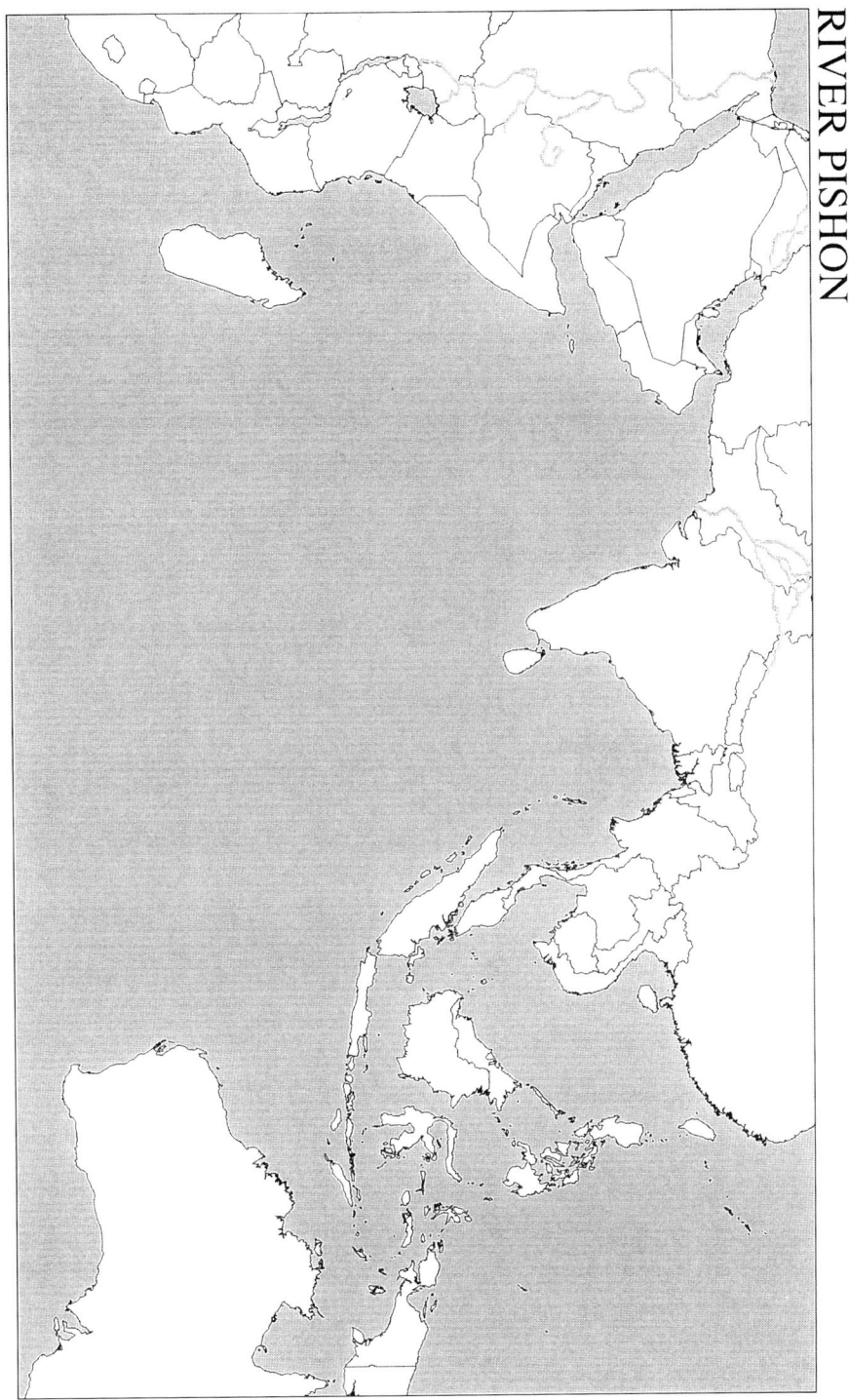

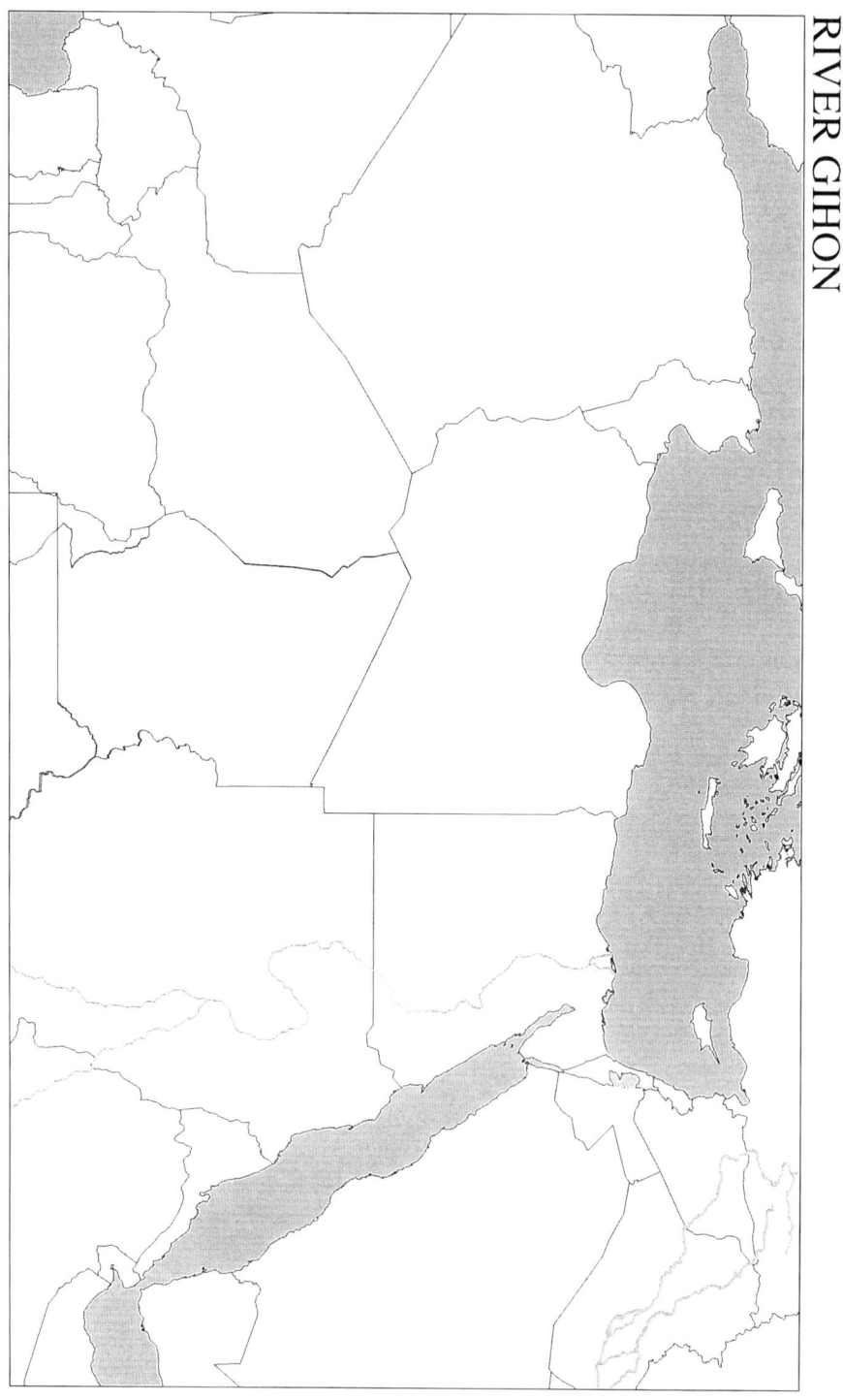

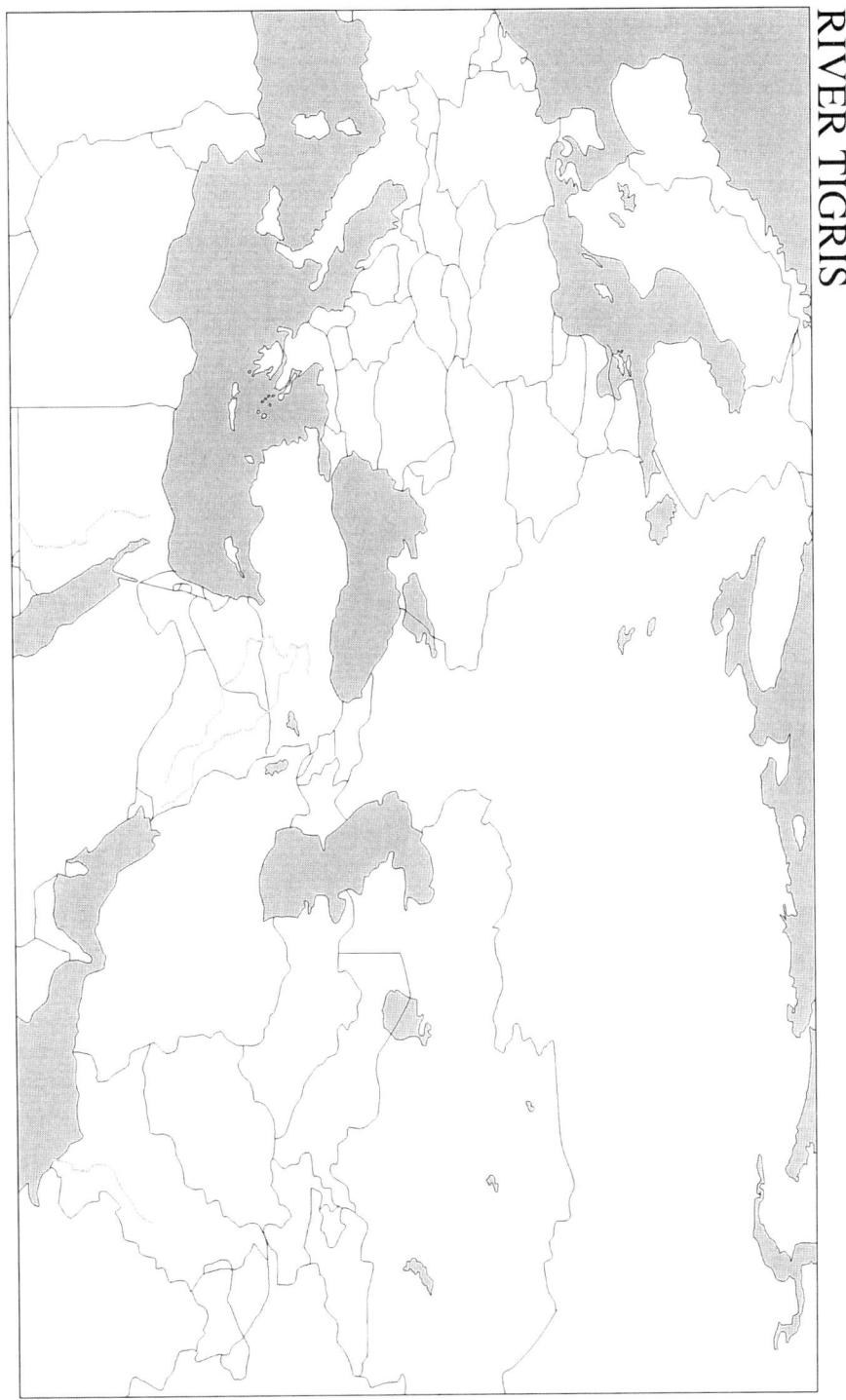

The Meaning of the Numbers of the Antichrist

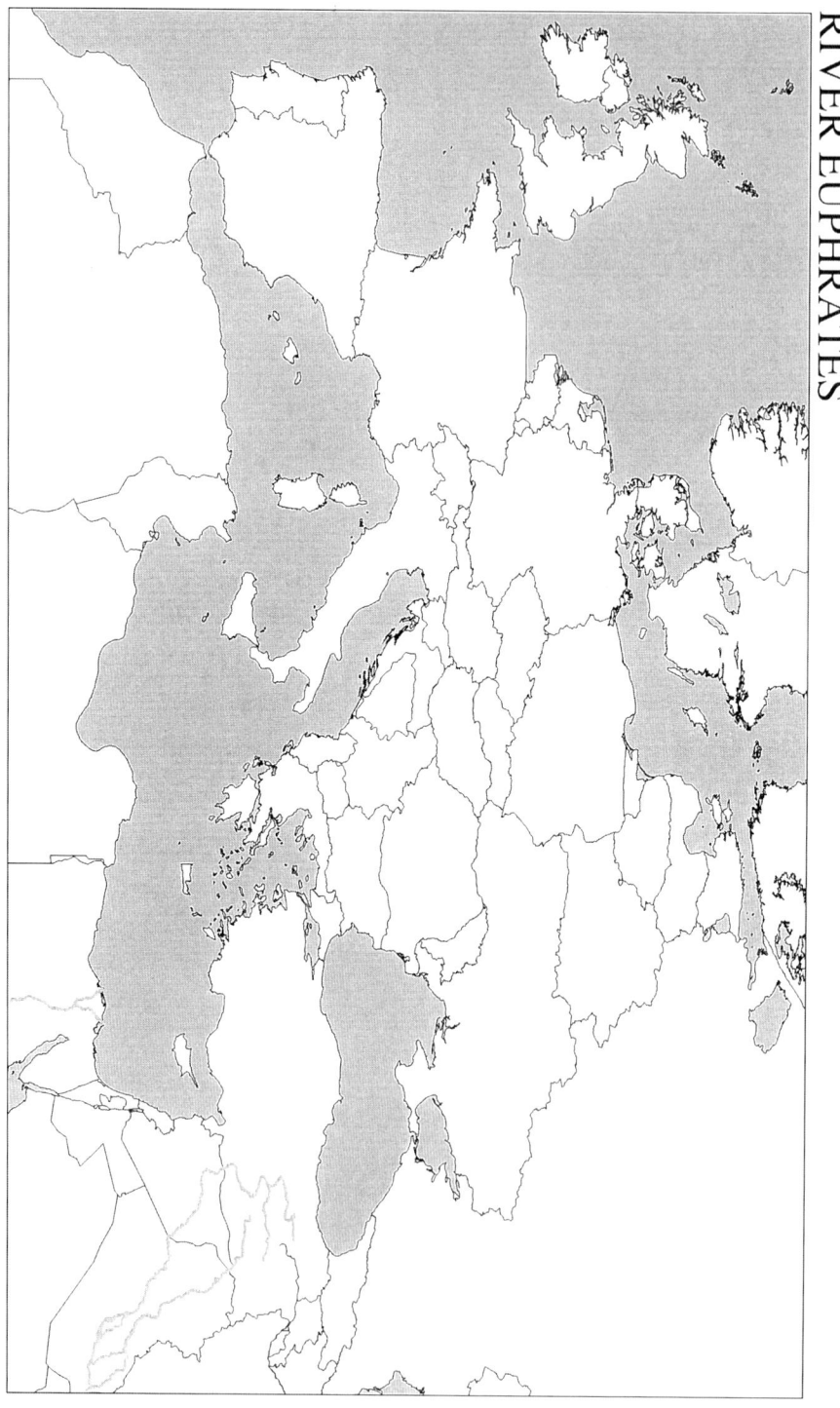

RIVER EUPHRATES

priests. Political leadership became complex. Local officials who functioned as city controllers were called *ensi*, meaning "governor for the gods." A kinglike figure was the *lugal*, literally translated as "big man." Scholars were either members of the priestly colleges or worked under their supervision in burgeoning temple complexes, alongside artists. The fabric of Mesopotamian civilization thus was woven in the form of a gradual expansion of preexisting institutions. In this process, women lost much of the influence they had exercised in barbaric villages.

Another characteristic of the civilized condition is the city. Census figures of 36,000, perhaps men only, have been discovered. Sumeria had become a land of competing city–states.

The Sumerian form of writing is designated *cuneiform*. It was developed from wedge-shaped symbols impressed on clay tablets. This technique came to be adopted by Elamites, Persians, Akkadians, Assyrians, Kassites, Hurrians, the Mitanni, Eblaites, and Hittites, each nation adapting it to its native tongue. Along routes of trade and conquest, Sumerian religion and scholarship became widely dispersed throughout the Fertile Crescent and beyond. Their language, like that of nearby Elam, is unrelated to any other, ancient or modern. Ancient Mesopotamia became known for its large, brick buildings called ziggurats. These buildings were really square or rectangular structures made of brick and built on top of each other to form a "step pyramid." One such edifice, which may have been reminiscent of the infamous Tower of Babel, contained seven levels, topped off by a temple-like structure representing an eighth. Ziggurats were the centerpieces of a complex of buildings utilized by the religious and secular officialdom. They were thought of as representing mountains.

There were many aspects to religion and scholarship. City rulers and kings commonly functioned as chief priests. The population worshiped a pantheon of gods and goddesses who possessed human characteristics and mythologies. The future was predicted by "haruspicy," which involved reading "signs" on the entrails of sacrificed animals, especially their livers. A mathematical system was developed with a base of sixty, which is why we still possess the conventions of sixty minutes to an hour, sixty seconds to a minute, and three hundred sixty degrees in a circle! Their calendar placed three hundred sixty days in a year. Leap periods were inserted at irregular intervals to keep the months in their proper season. Scholars conceived of words in a superstitious way. They thought one could capture and control the spirit or essence of a person or thing by merely remembering its name. Lists of supposed kings, going back more than seventy-two thousand years, were recited. As time went on, academic skills were valued more than practical achievements [12].

Experts find it hard to reconstruct the history of Sumeria because records were destroyed by repeated invasions. Hints of actual events can be gleaned from legends. The most important of these are about the epic hero Gilgamesh. In the legend of Gilgamesh and Agga, king Agga rules the city of Kish. He is the first king to come into power after the Great Flood. Gilgamesh builds (or rebuilds) the city of Uruk (also called Erech). Agga is captured when the young men of Uruk, led by Gilgamesh, successfully resist his attack. Recalling that Agga once did the same for him, Gilgamesh lets him go.

Much is recorded about the Great Flood in these stories. Seeking to speak with

The Meaning of the Numbers of the Antichrist

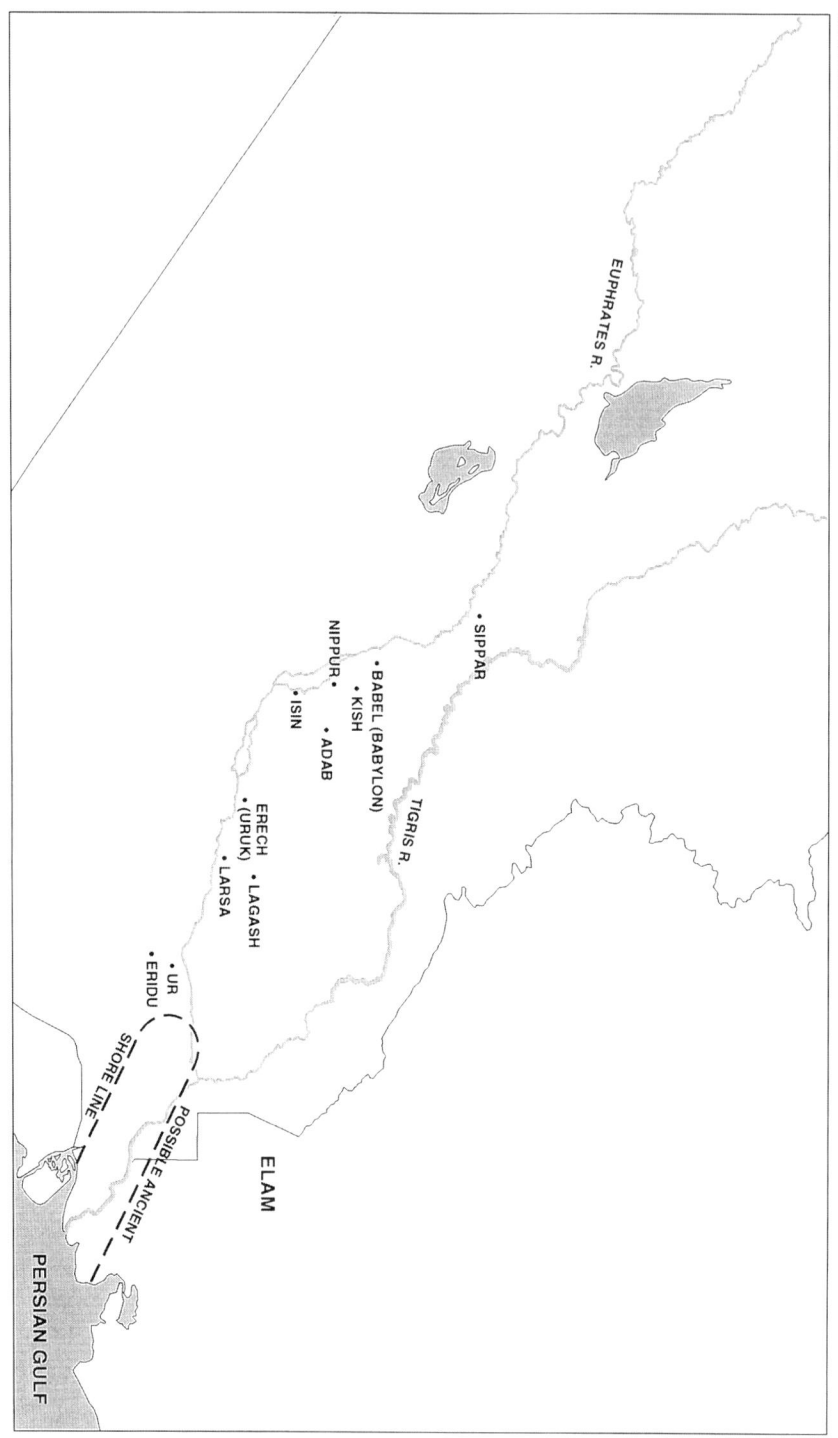

Utanapishtim, the Sumerian Noah, Gilgamesh makes a long and dangerous trip to the end of the earth. He is taken by ferry across the Waters of Death, where he has an audience with Utanapishtim, who relates his account of survival during the deluge. He, his family, and the animals were spared due to their obedience to God's instructions. The ark takes the shape of a cube in this version. When it was all over, Utanapishtim offered sacrifices. He and his wife were granted eternal life, and they settled down at the Mouth of the Rivers [13].

Surviving records mention a man named Enmebaragesi, Agga's father. A "wild man" with the title Enkidu was induced to come into Uruk. He made friends with Gilgamesh and shared many of his adventures. It is thought the real Gilgamesh lived about 2700–2600 B.C. [14]

The Myth of Atrahasis adds a spicy inside scoop. Irritated by noise and overpopulation, it seems the gods had long thought to diminish men, devising numerous devastations before finally deciding to do the job right by sending the Flood to wipe out the whole human race [15].

The Egyptian civilization arose a little after that in the Sumerian cities. Interestingly, there appears to have been a Mesopotamian connection tied to the city of Uruk. In prehistoric days artifacts from there became concentrated in Syria, then throughout the Nile Valley. After receiving the accouterments of civilization, the Egyptians adapted them in their own unique manner.

Unlike the city states in the East, development was rapid in Egypt. Early it divided into two regions. The more populated portion was in the south and was called Upper Egypt because it lay along the upper part of the Nile River. The Northern Country referred to the delta in the north. This portion remained a wilderness backwater for a long time. The first pharaoh was the legendary Menes, who united the two countries around 3150 B.C. Egypt was the world's first true nation. *Pharaoh* stood for "ruler of Egypt" and "lord of both countries." Another antediluvian pharaoh was named Narmer. The house of Pharaoh was, from the beginning, the most powerful institution in the land.

At its inception, Egypt was divided into territorial provinces known as *nomes*. A governor, called a *nomarch*, ruled each territory. Nomes became a remarkably long-lasting feature of Egyptian political life, and were not done away until the Arab invasion of 640 A.D.

The pharaohs soon came to be viewed as divine rulers, or "god-kings."

While it maintained trade up the coast of the Levant, this faraway land generally stayed aloof from international affairs. The Egyptians, during most of their history, were ancient isolationists. On only the rarest occasions was an Egyptian government toppled by an invasion of foreigners.

A notion of importance in Egypt was *ka,* or the eternal spirit of each person. Unlike in Mesopotamia, priesthoods and temples started out as small affairs. Only during the latter stages of the nation's history did some of the priests oversee great temple complexes or lead congregations that were large and powerful enough to influence the houses of the pharaohs and nomarchs. A sampling from their intricate system of deities could include Ra, a sun god, and Osiris, the ruler of the underworld who came to represent death and resurrection of the pharaohs. Osiris's wife, Isis, gained a sizeable cult following. Horus

The Meaning of the Numbers of the Antichrist

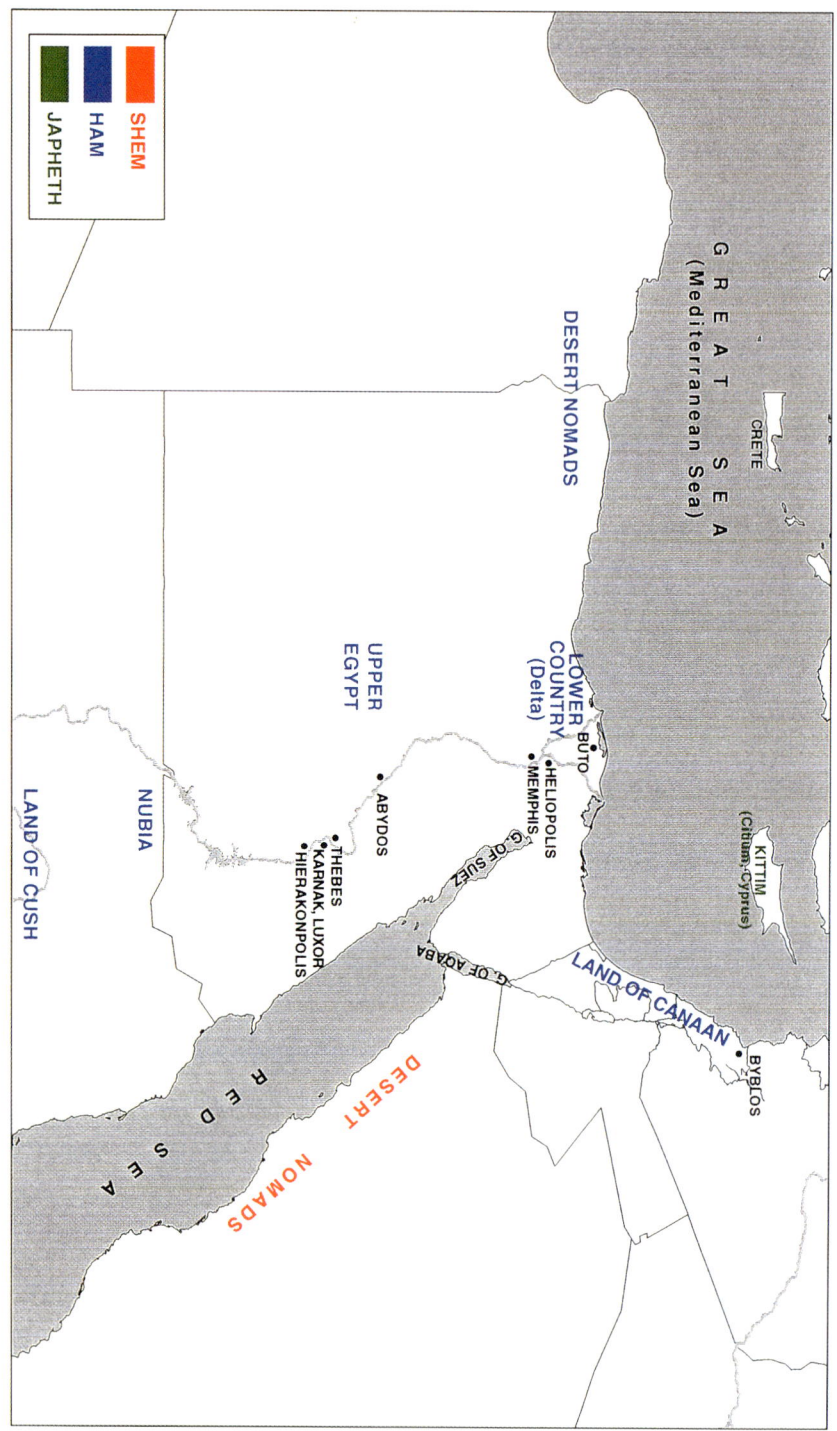

was a favorite god of the pharaohs, and they routinely adopted "Horus-names" upon assuming their office. Osiris's brother, Set, who was associated with the desert and its peoples, was a god of chaos and violence.

An individual could rise above his neighbors in Egypt if he obtained a good education. Endlessly discussing and recording every aspect of life, hordes of scribes found positions with the houses of pharaohs and the nomarchs or in temple institutions. Real academic accomplishment produced a number system with a base of ten, which is still used today. Their calendar accurately placed 365 days in a year.

Myths of Osiris and Isis relate a plot by the evil god, Set, in which he tricks Pharaoh Osiris into lying inside a large box. The box becomes his coffin when the top is treacherously nailed down. Set afloat on the Nile, the vessel finally comes to rest in the Canaanite city of Byblos. Fascinating in this regard are details to be read in the biblical account of the Great Flood which provide the dimensions of Noah's ark. Its dimensions were equivalent to those of a coffin.

A meaningful spiritual icon understood by these people was known as "the eye of Horus [16]."

Nations speaking the languages of Semites finally put an end to the ancient Sumerians [17]. Yet we today continue to keep alive phrases such as "a human tide" or "flood" to depict unstoppable movements of people and ideas.

Very early in Egyptian history two controversial pharaohs of the second dynasty took names associated with Set, as well as the already traditional Horus names. But their policy came to be rejected in favor of the original practice. Meanwhile in Shinar, the Early Dynastic Period I collapsed at roughly the same time: 2800–2700 B.C. [18]

The *gopher wood* in the book of *Genesis* is thought to refer to the cypress tree. The only notable thing about cypress is that its wood is so hard and knotty it is thought to be useless. Noah and his boys made their storied craft with materials considered of no value to this world [19].

The name *Nimrod* means "subduer of the leopard" or, simply, "leopard." After Babel, he is said to have built Erech (Uruk) and two more cities in the south before founding the settlements that soon after were united to form Assyria. Researchers add that an ethnic group to the north, the Subarians, gained a presence in Mesopotamia [20]. "*Nephilim, or giant*, means "a bully or tyrant," or "feller" (as in felling trees) [21].

The Fertile Crescent foothills and the valley of the Nile River in Egypt had been heavily deforested by early in the Bronze Age. They say dates are accurate to the century.

THE MEANING OF THE NUMBERS OF THE ANTICHRIST

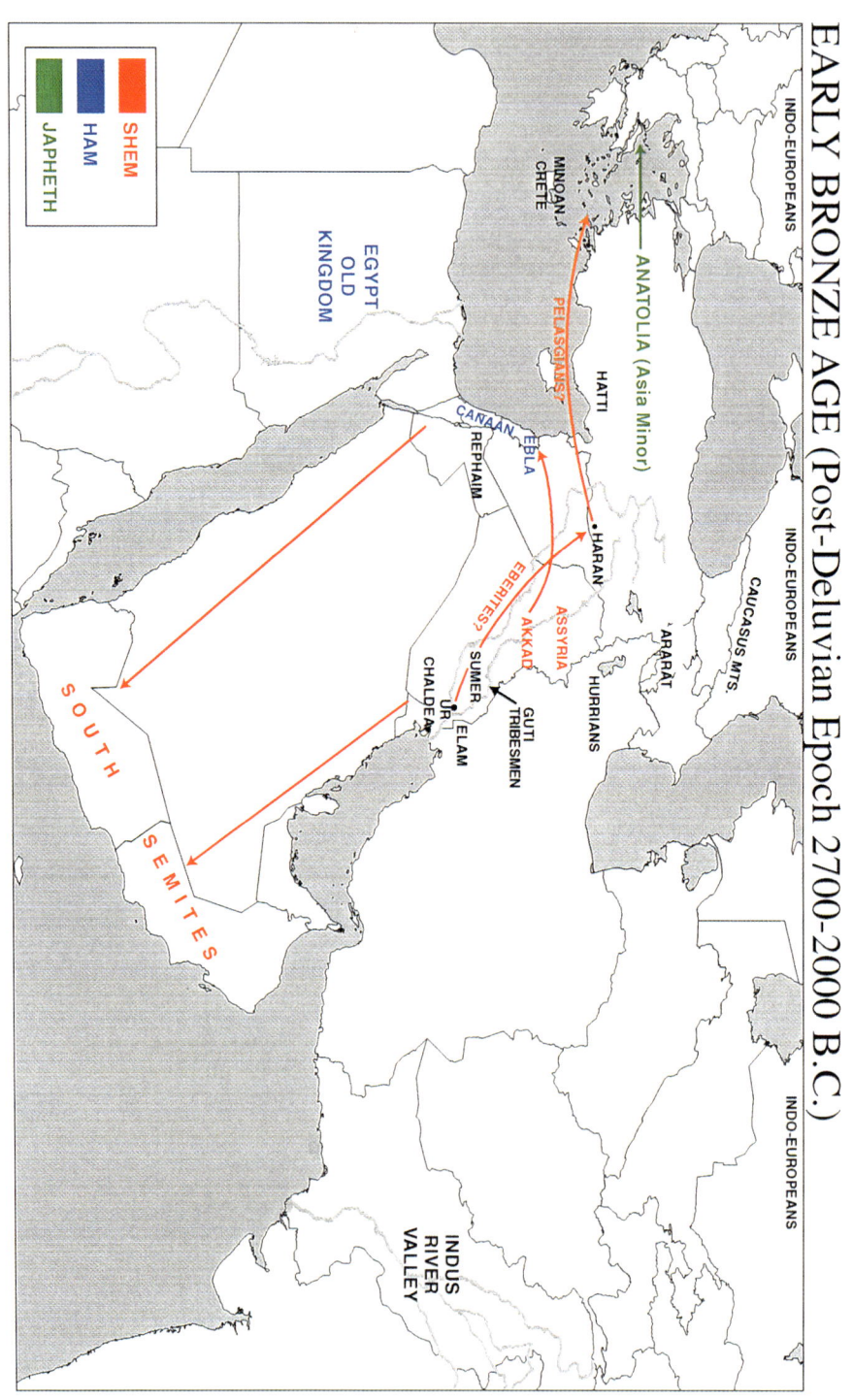

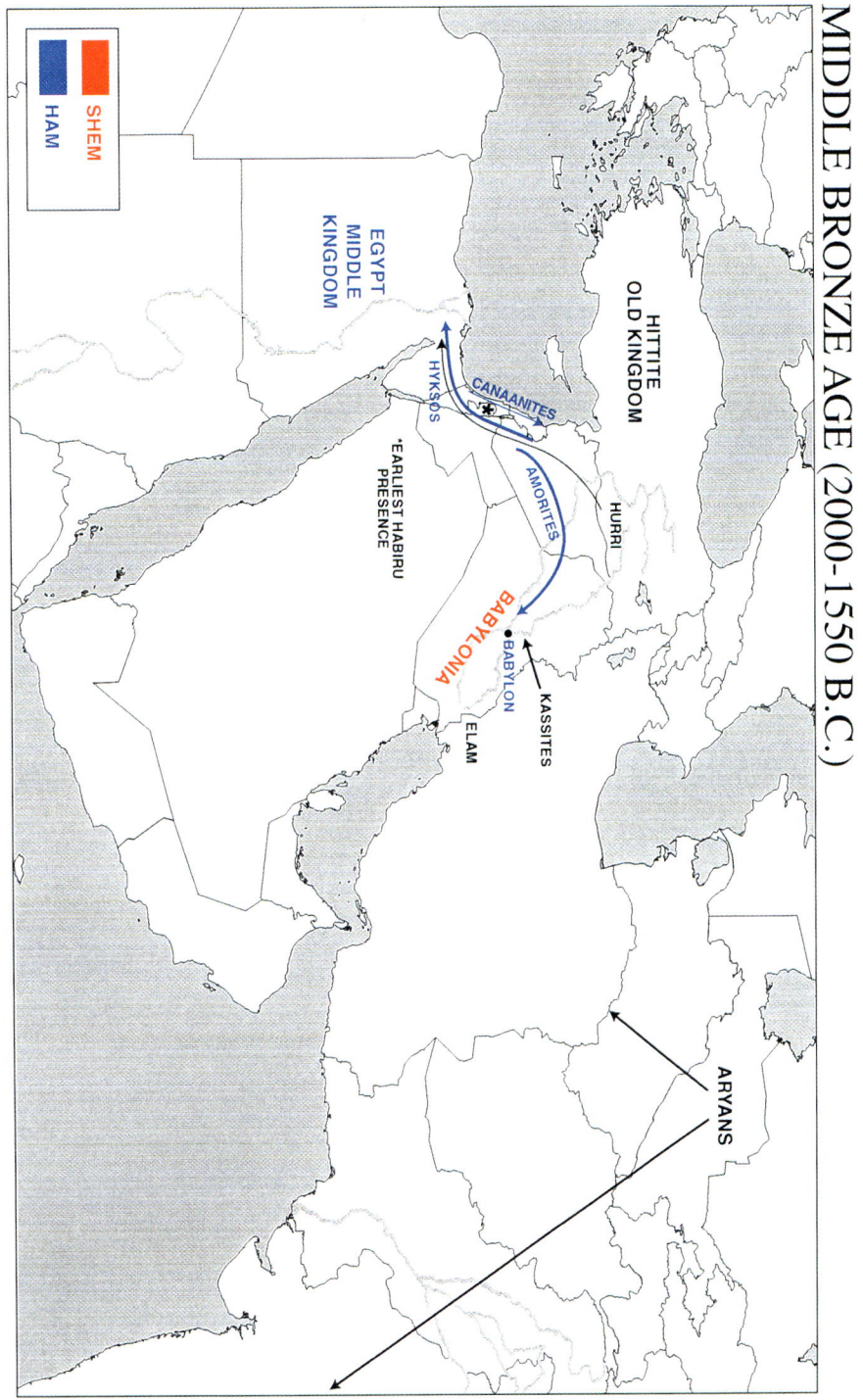

References

1. Genesis 1:1-2:3

2. Daniel 8:2

3. Isaiah 14:12-14; Ezekiel 28:11-18; Genesis 4:14b, 15; 1 Kings 18:1-44

4. Genesis 2:18-25; 4:25-5:32

5. Genesis 4:1-8

6. Genesis 2:11-14

7. Genesis 1:21, 24, 28; 2:7, 19; 3:20; 6:19; 8:1, 17, 21; 9:10, 12, 15, 16
   Genesis 1:24, 25, 30; 2:19, 20; 3:1, 14; 7:14, 21; 8:19; 9:2, 5, 10x2

8. Genesis 3:1-6

9. Genesis 2:15-17

10. Genesis 2:4-10; 3:22, 23

11. Genesis 4:16-24

12. Genesis 3:12-21

13. Genesis 9:28, 29

14. Genesis 10:8b-12

15. Genesis 6:9-9:17

16. Genesis 6:15-16; 12:1-10; 9:18-27?

17. Genesis 11:10-32

18. Psalm 32

19. Genesis 6:13-14; 7:1-5

20. Genesis 7:6-9:17; 1 Peter 3:17-22; 1 Corinthians 10:1-13; Psalm 29

21. Genesis 6:4b; 10:1-32; Joshua 1:1-9

Chapter Two
Expansion of Civilization

Most of the civilized world entered a dark age following the invasions of *sea people,* who demolished the Hittite Empire after 1200 B.C. [1] In time, two great Hamito-Semitic Iron Age empires emerged. These were the neo-Assyrian Empire and the neo-Babylonian empire.

It was in this period that ancient Israel was rent in two. [2] The northern half, named the Kingdom of Israel, was crushed and its people forcibly relocated eastward by the hand of Assyria in 721 B.C. Never returning en mass to Palestine, their whereabouts have become shrouded in mystery. Yet their legacy endures under the standard of a haunting epithet, "The Ten Lost Tribes of Israel. [3]" The Kingdom of Judah, to the south, consisted primarily of two tribes with a large remnant of a third. Judah, to which the kings belonged, was the most numerous of the twelve Hebrew tribal groups. The word "Jew" is a derivative of the word "Judah." The small tribe of Benjamin stuck with its Jewish brethren following the division of the nation, which took place around 900 B.C. Although chosen as the seat of government by Judaic kings, the city of Jerusalem actually lay in Benjamite territory. A number of Israel's ancient priests from the tribe of Levi dwelt in Judah's territory after the dividing of the country [4]. The captivity of the people of Judah, which began in 605 B.C., took place in the time of the neo-Babylonian empire under Nebuchadnezzar II, the Great [5]. Beginning seventy years later, some of the people returned under the auspices of Persian kings [6]. Nehemiah, a levitical priest, was later appointed to oversee the rebuilding of the wall around Jerusalem [7].

Thus, *Old Testament* Israel, from the Middle Bronze Age, made its stand between a network of small but highly advanced nations clustered near the Tigris and Euphrates rivers and wealthy Egypt to its south. Marching along the Fertile Crescent, armies from the former would at times swoop in *from the north* [8]. Any strongman who stood up in these regions might have qualified as another biblical *king of the north*. The biblical *king of the south* designated the pharaoh, King of Egypt [9].

People speaking Indo-European languages expanded from a nomad culture in prehistoric Central Asia. Early, these tribes divided into two branches. Within the Indo branch were the legendary Aryans, who invaded the Indus Valley civilization before moving into India itself. An offshoot of warriors known as the Mitanni set up their kingdom in the extreme north of Mesopotamia. Other Aryan tribal confederations, which came to be known as Medes and Persians, infiltrated into modern Iran. The name *Iran* means "land of the Aryans." Gotama the Buddha, born near the border of present-day Nepal and India, lived between 600 and 400 B.C.

The European branch of Indo-Europeans included the Slavs, who entered eastern Europe from Asia early in historical times. Scandinavians were influenced by trade and its resulting contacts along the rivers leading to the Baltic Sea from the Black and Caspian Seas. The culture of Celtic tribes once dominated much of eastern and western Europe as far as the British Isles and Ireland. *Germanic* was the name applied to Scandinavians who moved south into central and eastern Europe. Numerous other groups were scattered through southern Europe.

Japheth, one of the sons of Noah, instigated a northward migration following the Great Flood. Those who followed were instrumental in developing scattered "isles" of frontier settlements around Indo-European territories [10].

Indo-Europeans made another major encroachment upon the civilized Near Eastern world in 559 B.C., when the Medes and Persians toppled the neo-Babylonian empire [11]. They maintained the vast Achaemenian Dynasty until 330 B.C. A closely related group set up Parthian kingdoms from 247 B.C. until 224 A.D., which was during Roman times. A peace treaty between the two was signed in 92 B.C. Its terms were that the Parthian kings were free to take what they could rule east of the Euphrates River, whereas Rome was given all the lands it could assimilate from the Euphrates to the West. While they engaged in subsequent wars, this arrangement usually held firm through the subsequent histories of both powers. It was the decentralized Parthians who set the eastern limit of the Roman Empire [12]. A Sasanian dynasty, of Persian heritage, was established in 224 A.D.

Through trade, colonization of Anatolian coastal lands, and the adventures of the Greco-Persian Wars, the Greeks had made themselves known in the Near East. In 337 B.C., a man named Philip II of Macedon organized among Grecian cities a league for mutual defense called the "League of Corinth." It was joined by all the city-states except Sparta. Philip had come from Macedonia, which was to the immediate north of Greece, and his organization sponsored the armies of his son, Alexander the Great.

Considered the most brilliant and successful military commander ever to take the field, Alexander, with his men, conquered all of the civilized world to the doors of India and the Far East. In their final campaign, they trekked as far as the Indus River valley in modern Pakistan. There, they defeated the forces of a king named Porus. Afterwards, Porus, who cultivated a relationship of mutual respect with the young commander and his people, aligned his kingdom toward the Near East and West rather than with India when he accepted Greek hegemony.

Upon placing his throne in Babylon, the new emperor busied himself planning sea trade with India and sending officers on a northern expedition to explore the Caspian Sea. He received congratulatory delegations from as far away as Libya and Italy! By means of trade, commerce, and cultural exchange, Alexander was working to build the city of Babylon into a global capital when he unexpectedly caught a fever and died at the age of thirty-three.

As predicted, his territories were divided by four eminent officers. General Cassander returned home, where he seized Macedonia, the city of Athens and most of the rest of Greece. Kidnapping her son, Alexander IV, he forced the widow of Alexander, Roxana, into a political marriage.

Seleucus I Nicator picked out the governorship, or satrapy, of Babylon. Ptolemy I Soter chose to be the satrap of Egypt, Libya, and Arabia. A talented bodyguard named Lysimachus received the governorship of Thrace; however, a fifth figure, Antigonus I

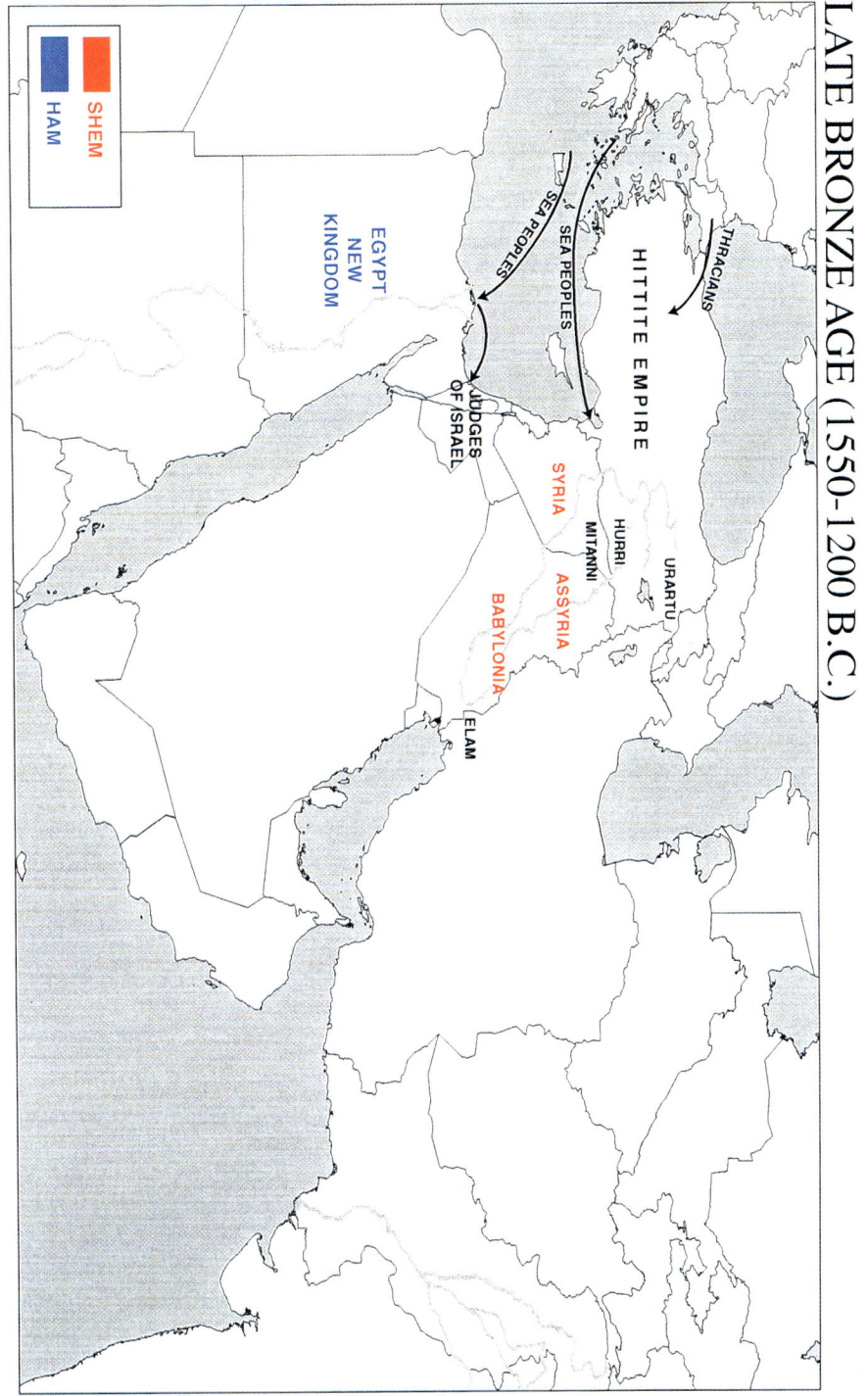

The Meaning of the Numbers of the Antichrist

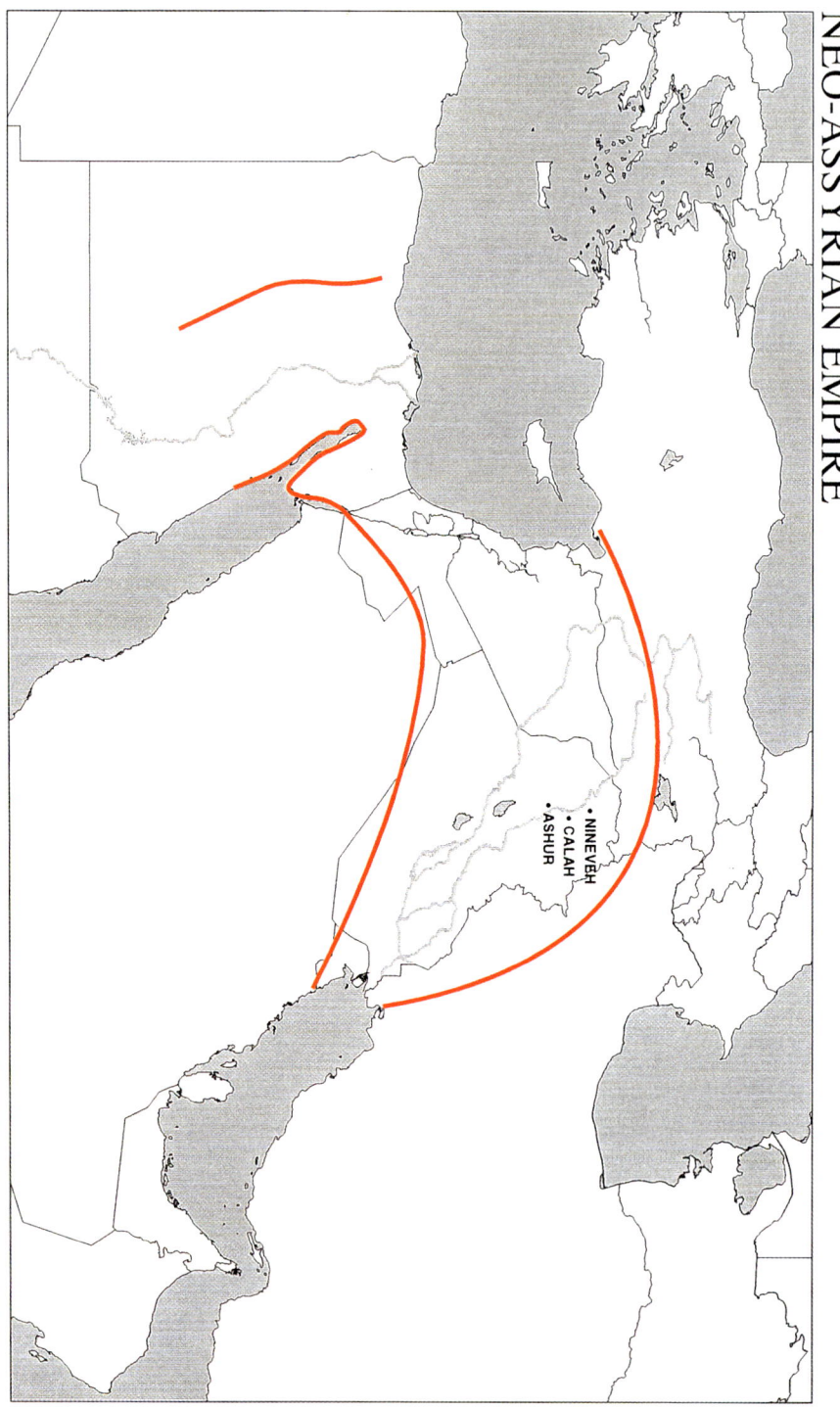

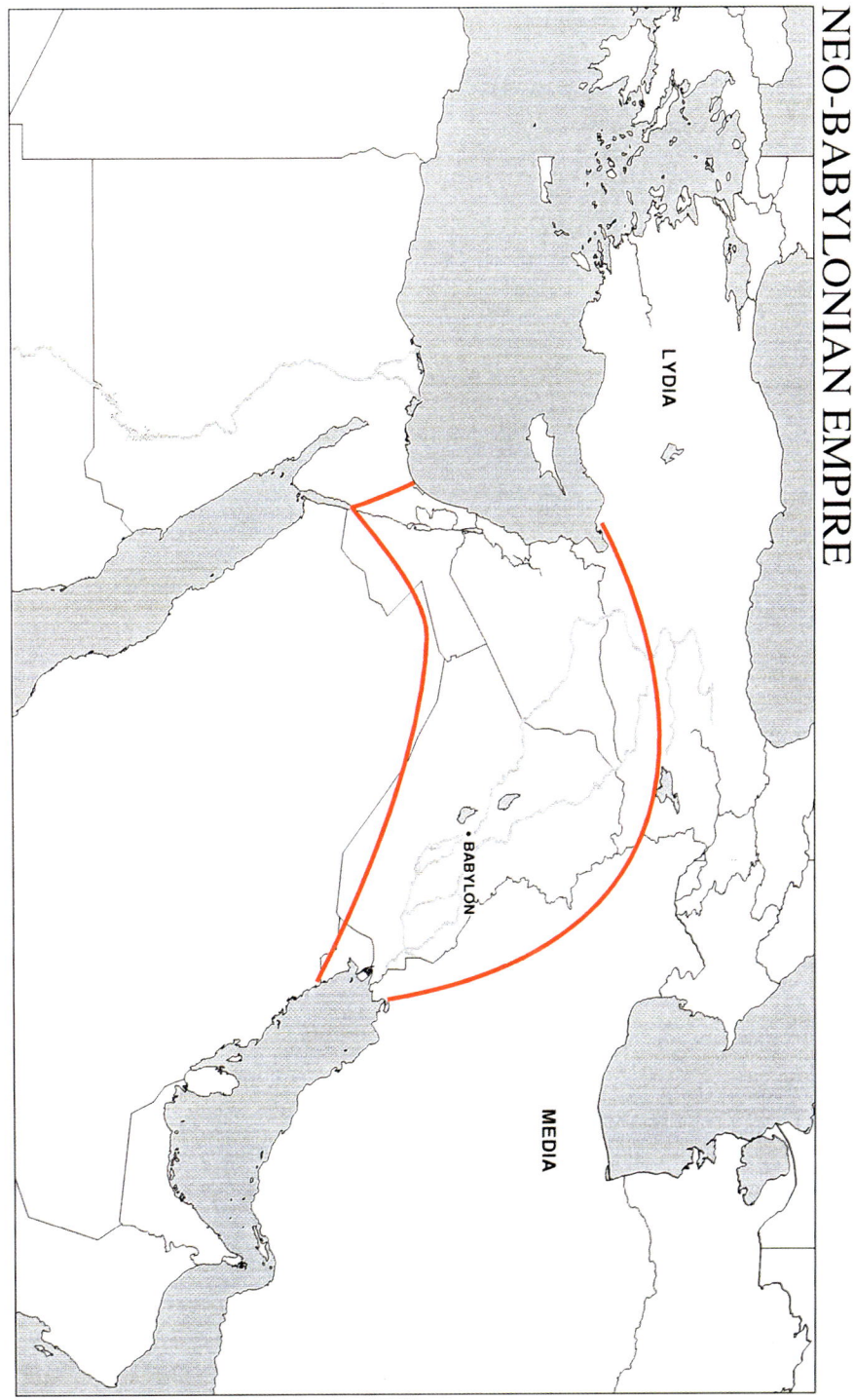

The Meaning of the Numbers of the Antichrist

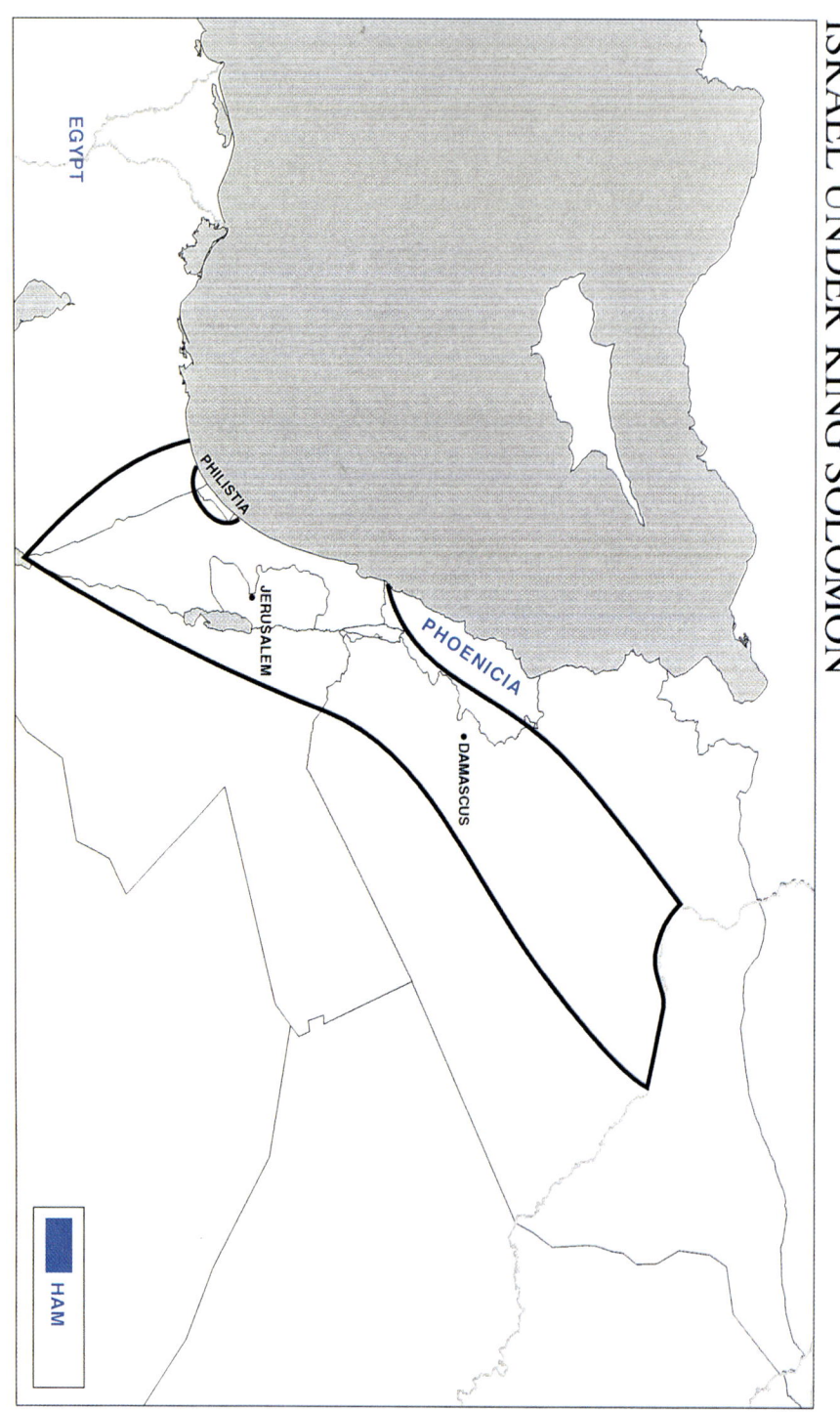

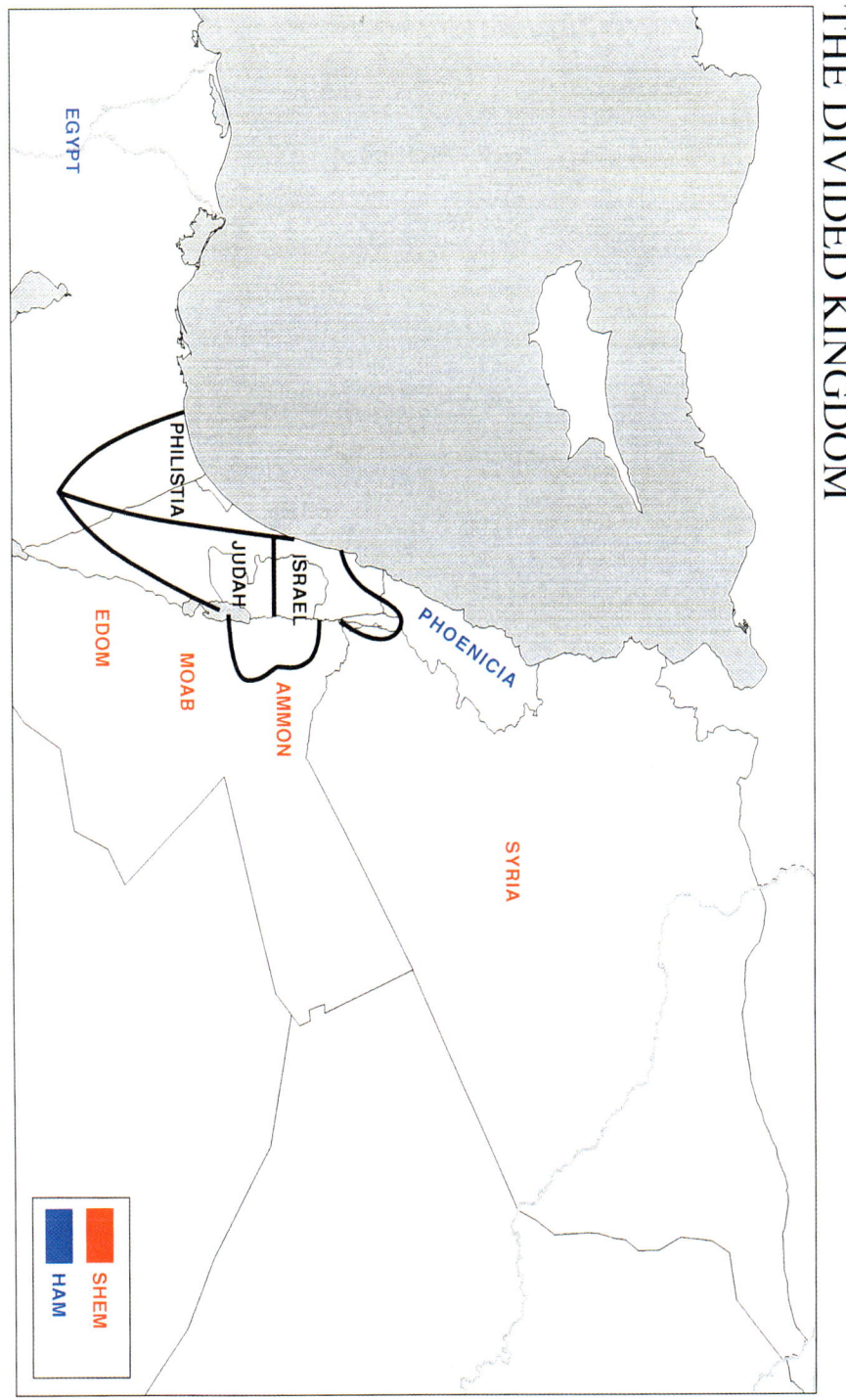

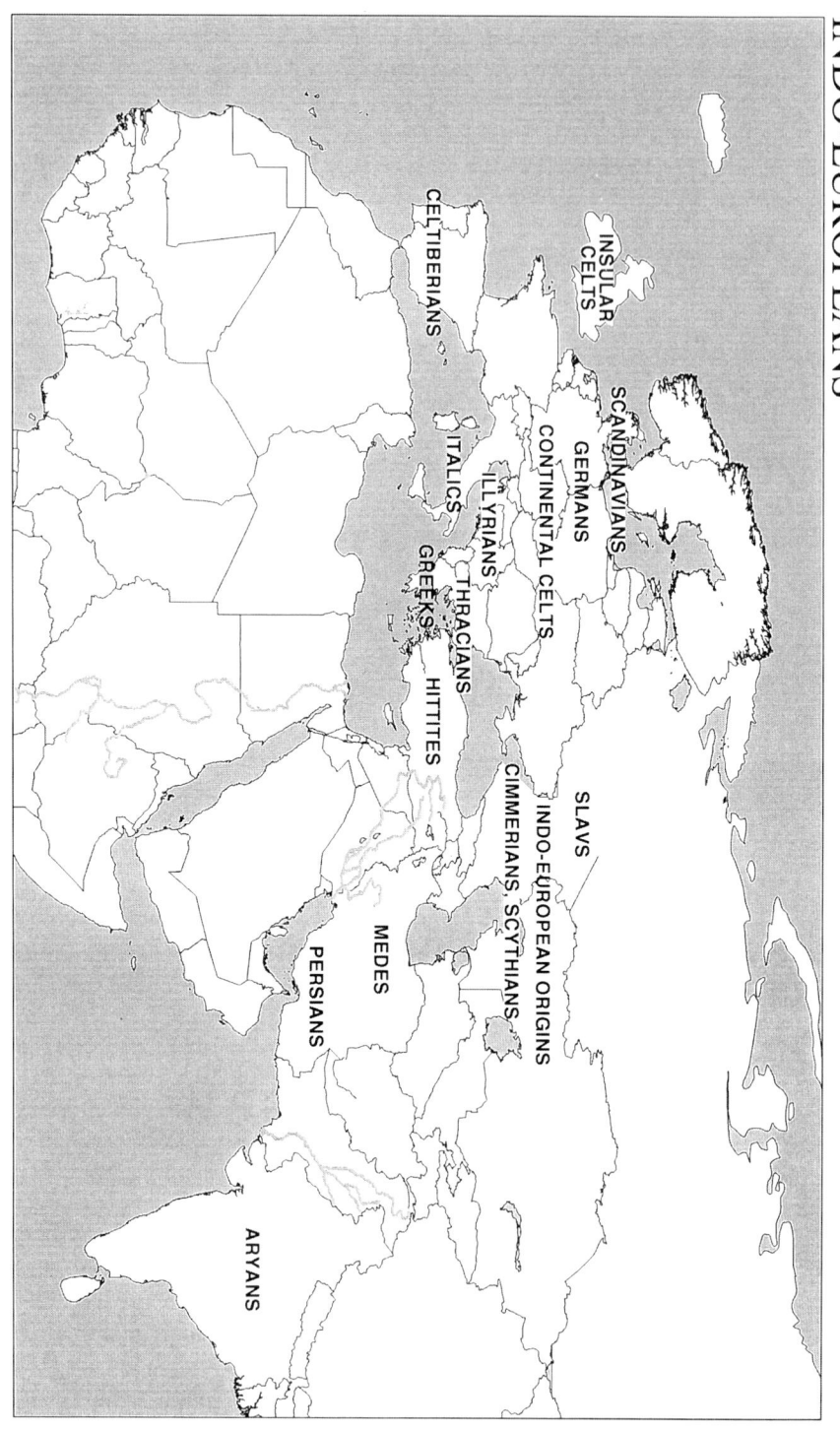

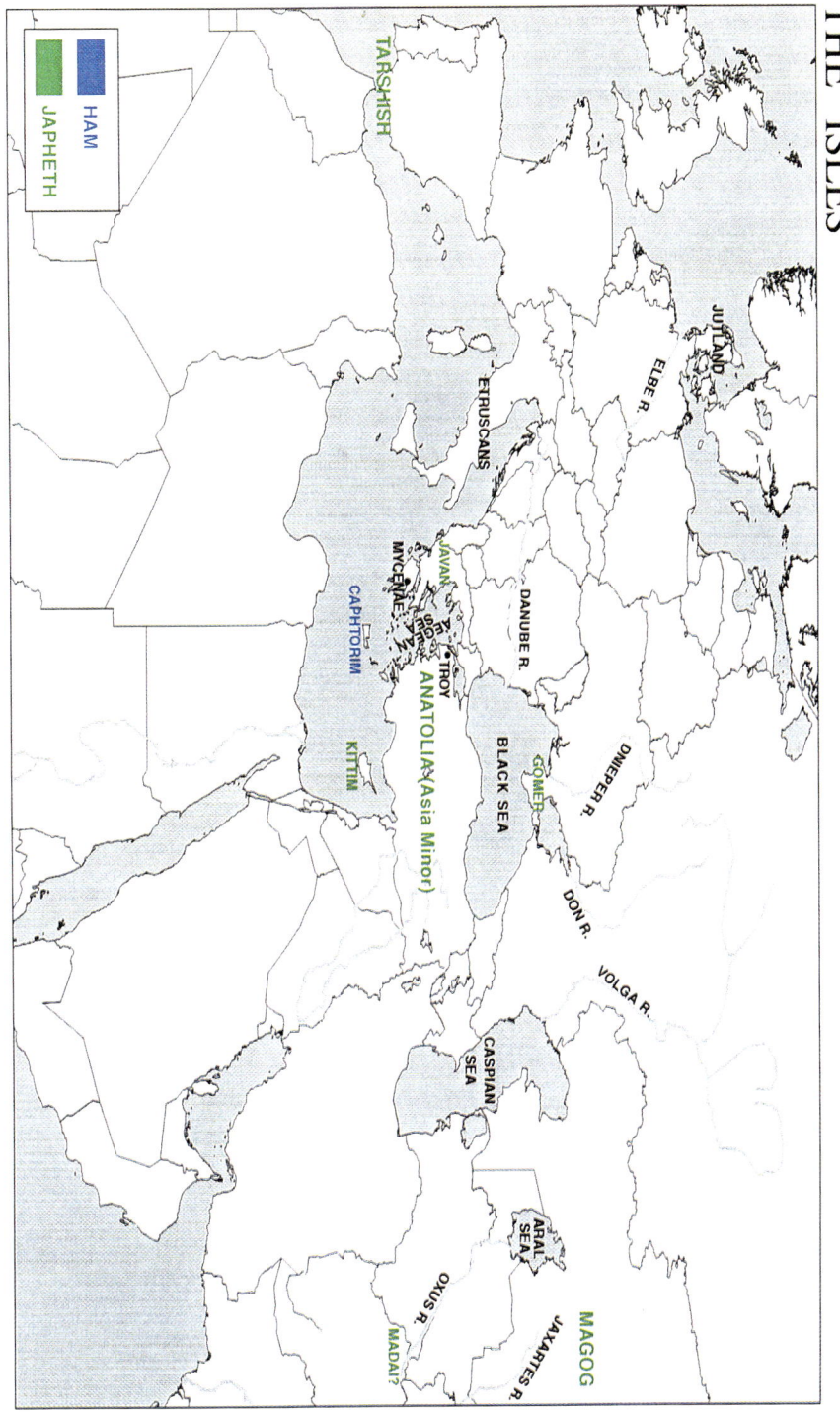

Monophthalmus, maintained intentions of reuniting the whole empire under his rule. From a base in Asia Minor, he moved to attack the defenses of Cassander in Greece. Known to have always hated Alexander the Great, the general was forced to retreat to Macedonia, where he became a narrow and bitter man. He had Roxana and Alexander IV murdered on the way. Ultimately, Antigonus was defeated as well, and Seleucus and Ptolemy founded large empires. Lysimachus was able to add most of Anatolia to his substantial possessions.

Following the example of their visionary forefathers, Grecians in the Near East adapted themselves to the customs and institutions of the surrounding people. With their rich language and arts as stimuli, the international cooperation that followed produced the Hellenistic Age [13].

It was Plato who founded the world's first true university in 387 B.C.

Buddhism came to be accepted much more in the Far East than in India or the Indus Valley, although it persists in India to this day in a form called Jainism.

The first civilization established on the Italian peninsula was that of the Etruscans. They initiated an array of foreign contacts that came to include Assyria, Urartu, Syria, Anatolia, the Caucasus, Greece, Phoenicia and Carthage, and Egypt. Etruscan priests became famed augurs. Like the Chaldeas of a prior era, they peered into the proscribed excesses of haruspicy. Incorporated from Indo-Europeans, the word "haruspex" referred to an Etruscan diviner. It has etymological connections with *hira*, Sanskrit for "entrails." In the Latin translation of the *Old Testament*, the name of the notorious Mesopotamian prophet, *Balaam* is written as *hariolus*, which meant "wizard" or "soothsayer."

The Romans obtained much of their government, religion, and culture from Etruscan neighbors and predecessors. A body of sixty Etruscan diviners continued to practice their methods of augury under Latin rule [14].

Starting with the nearby Sabines, this Italian tribe, whose main city sat on the Tiber River, implemented a brilliant and simple technique early in its ascendancy. In a manner that was carefully controlled, Rome offered the economic, political, and social advantages of citizenship to outsiders. Before long, the Romans had not only eclipsed the well-established Etruscans, they had united tribal groups through the whole of Italy into their state. This policy continued to be applied as they extended their empire into foreign lands.

The story of Rome's expansion into Asia centers on the person of Antiochus III, the Great. Having raised the Seleucid empire to its pinnacle, he proceeded to create a uniform administration for every province in order to keep himself firmly in control. He lived to see the loss of almost everything he had worked to achieve as former allies in Greece and Asia Minor turned away from him. The Roman Empire, which was already encroaching into Macedonia while in the process of defeating the empire of Carthage, was quick to take advantage [15].

Religious belief was an indispensable element of these developments. Because they stood between the majority of the people and the gods, Roman priests were prominent in most affairs of state. They were divided into four prestigious bodies. The *pontifices* became the most powerful of these. Divination was the *augures'* forte. Regulation of foreign cults was overseen by the officials of an institution called the *quindecimviri sacris faciundis*. Religious festivals were planned and supervised by the Epulones. The nation's

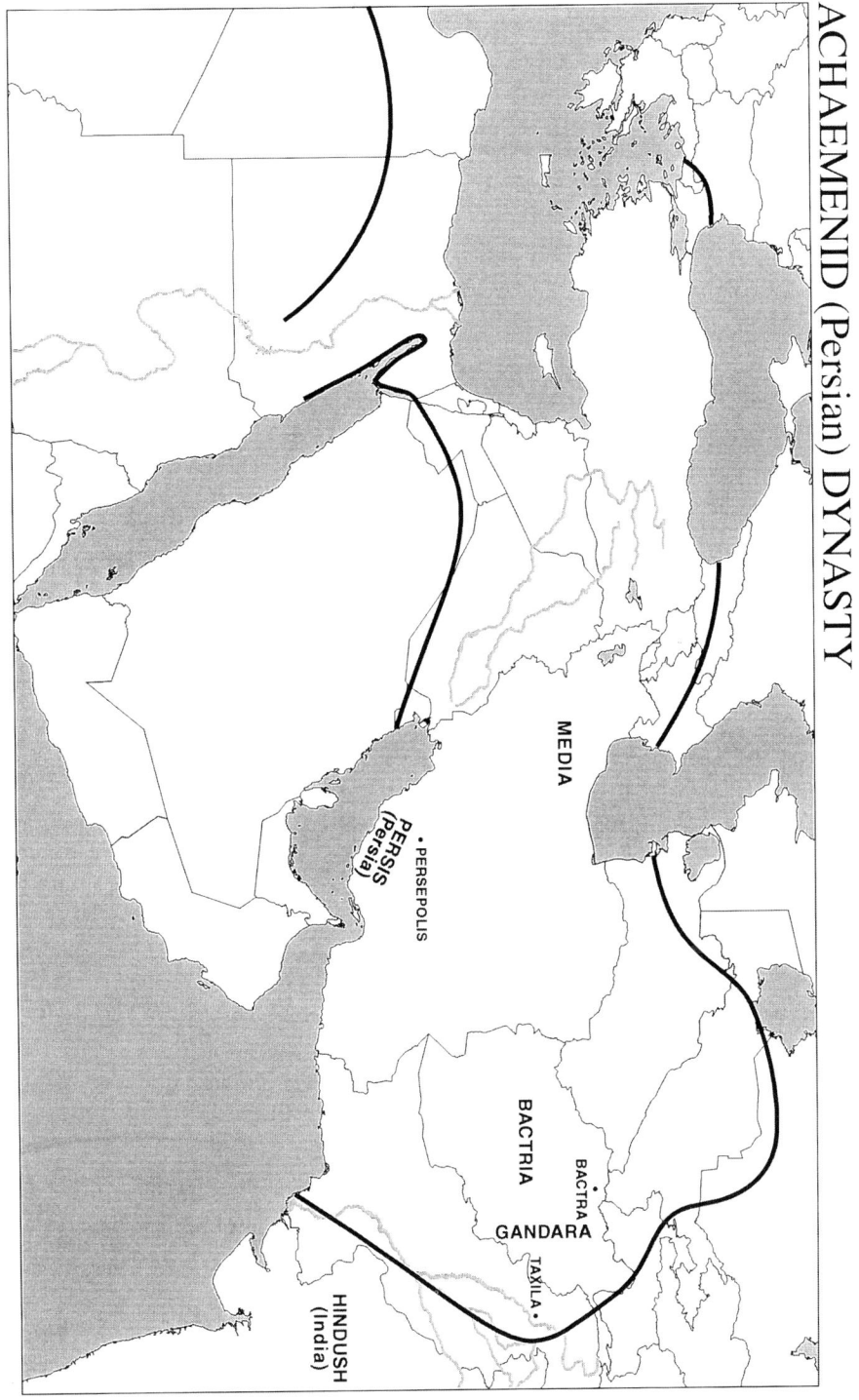

THE MEANING OF THE NUMBERS OF THE ANTICHRIST

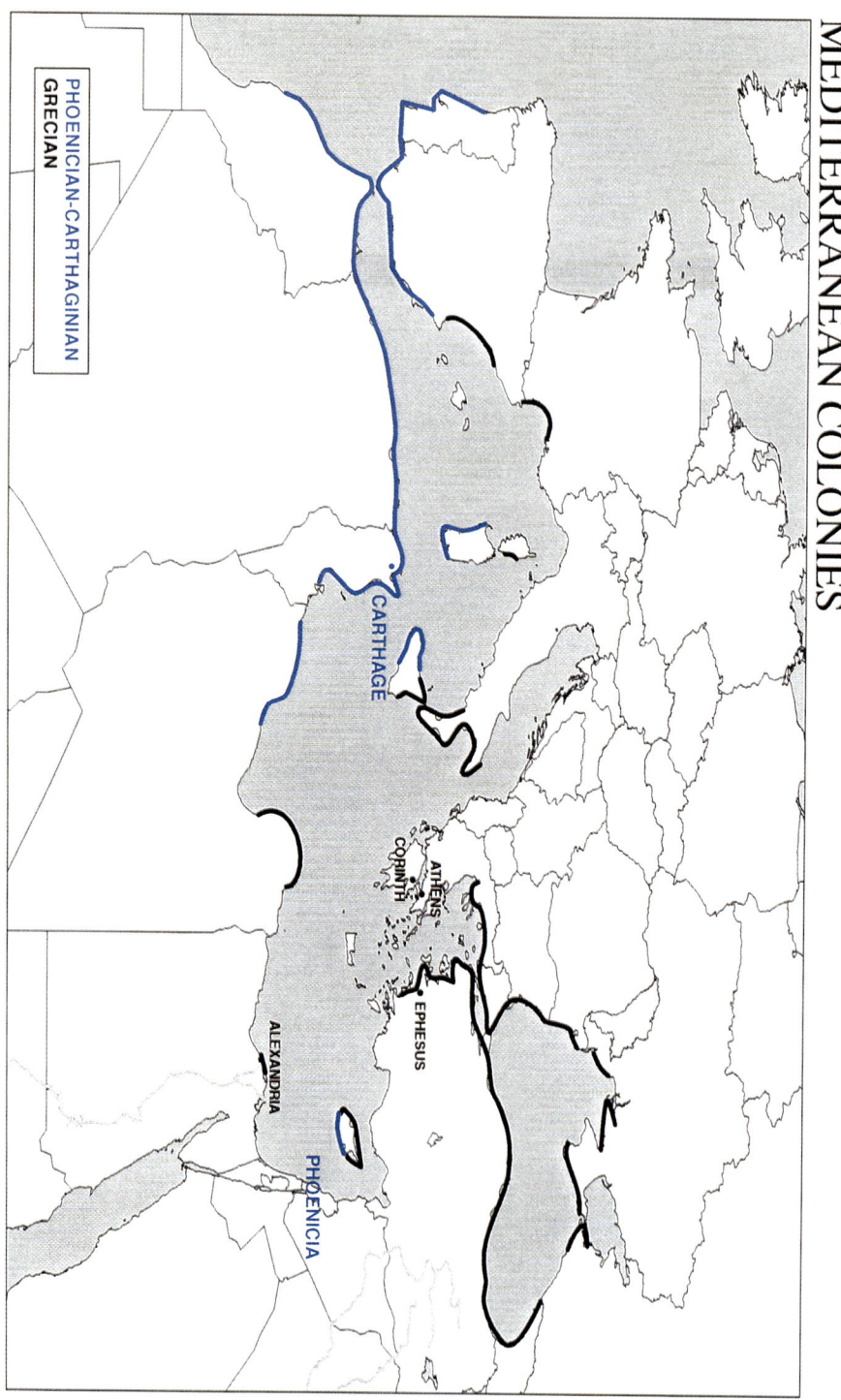

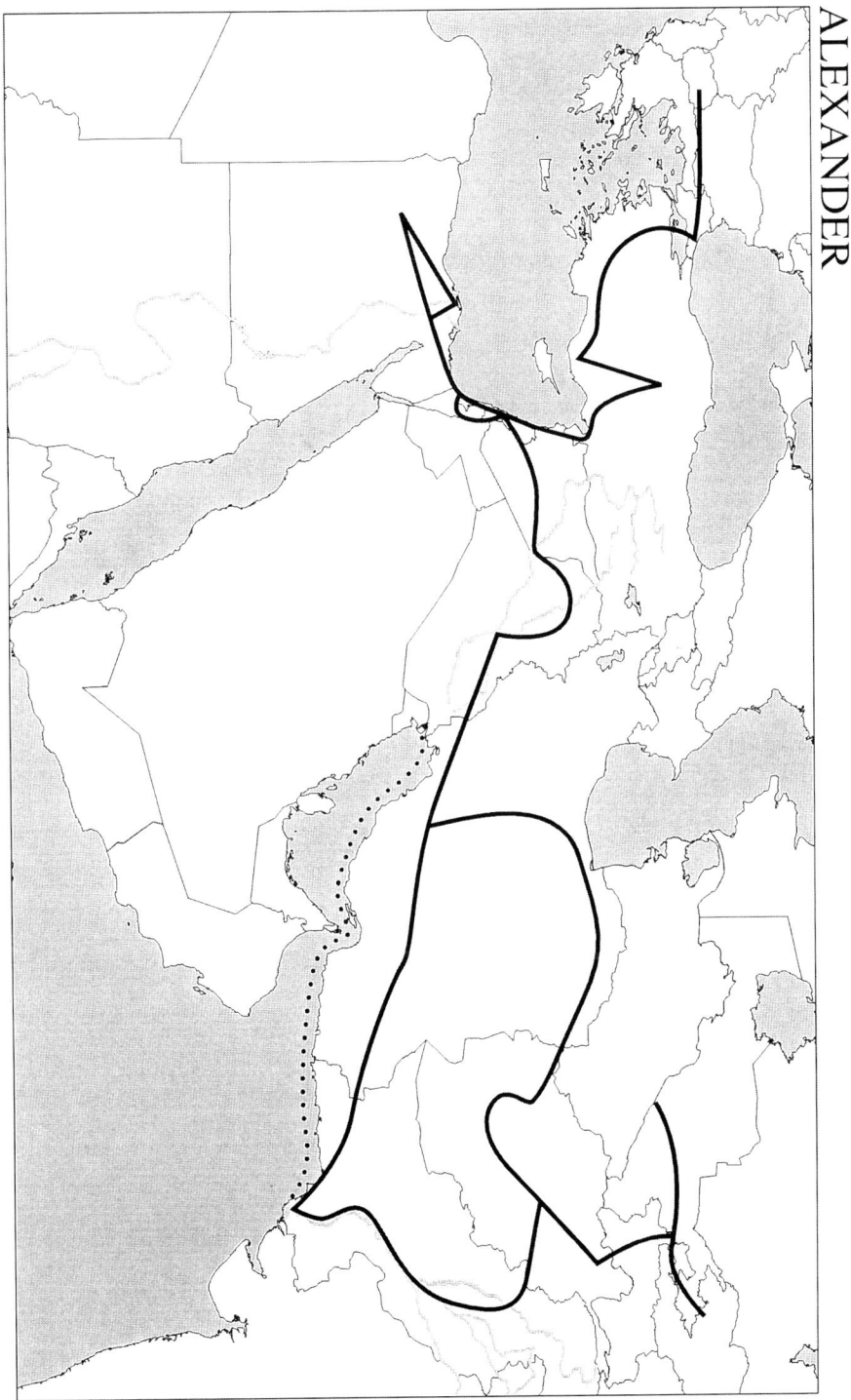

THE MEANING OF THE NUMBERS OF THE ANTICHRIST

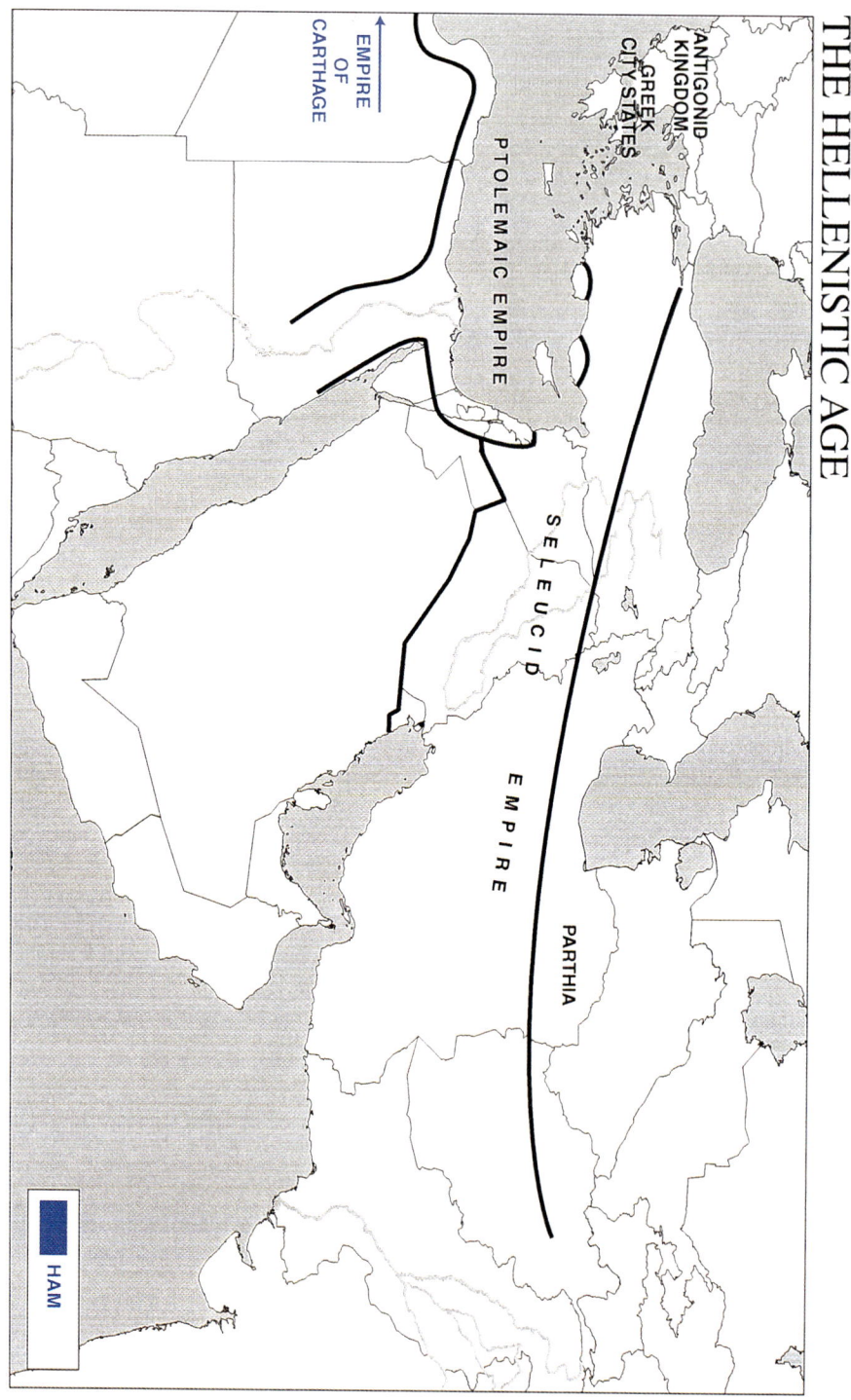

chief priest, who presided over the college of pontifices, held the title *pontifex maximus*. The office came to be assumed by the emperors, starting with Julius Caesar.

Responsibility for tending the fire of Vesta rested with the Vestal Virgins. Yet another agency, the *fetiales*, exercised ministration of treaties with foreign governments and declarations of war.

Traditional Roman religion, like that of the Etruscans, concerned itself with scrupulously observing rituals in order to please and placate the gods. Unlike the Greeks, the Romans did not develop a pantheon full of divinities possessing mythologies and human-like personalities. Romans believed that pious adherence to sacred protocol by their orderly system priests, along with the devoutness and self-sacrifice of the citizenry, so pleased the powers of heaven that the gods and goddesses had allowed them to dominate their world.

Yet the populace became dissatisfied with these notions, preferring to characterize their nation's history as having been too rigid and austere. In time, many eastern cults gravitated to Rome. These included the Egyptian goddess Isis; Attis, who was the consort of the Great Mother of Phrygia in Asia Minor; an Asian type of sun worship that was associated with the Syrian baal god; and a god from as far as Persia, who was known as Mithra.

Three multicultural Golden Ages have been seen to come and go during the ages of this world. The first was the Golden Age of Babel. It was pronounced broken up, by my reckoning, 101 years following the Great Flood [16]. The second Golden Age was inaugurated in Babylon during the reign of Nebuchadnezzar II, the Great, and lasted through the Persian Achaemenian Dynasty. As we have seen, it splintered abruptly with the death of Alexander in 323 B.C. [17] The Golden Age of Rome reached its height during the reigns of "five good emperors," beginning in 96 A.D. It slid immediately into a slow decline as the Roman world began to succumb to Christianity at its inception. A greater degree of cultural fusion and uniformity between a staggering list of far-flung religions, ethnic groups, and nations materialized at this time than in any age until the latter half of the twentieth century [18].

At least three events transpired in the year 93 A.D. which, when traced out and pondered, lead one into understanding at the dawn of a Golden Age [19].

A curious phenomenon took root toward the latter years of Rome's Golden Age. It became known as the Second Sophistic Movement. Numerous people, mostly of average means, sought to obtain a higher education. To their credit, they studied for years to gain their degrees. In order to qualify as a sophist, one had then to meet additional requirements in communication skills described as rhetoric. Lacking much practical knowledge, most were obliged to parlay their academic accomplishments into ways of making a living. An intricate network evolved, which linked academic institutions to government at all levels. A woman named Julia Domna, who served as empress during the reigns of her two sons, became a benefactor of these Roman sophists [20].

A middle class swelled as never before inside the Roman Empire. From its ranks appeared the literate carpenter, Jesus of Nazareth. Steering the gust of a sort of non-violent populist movement, he arrived at the capital city of Judaea with the eery awareness that a claim of sacred kingship must only be met by a rejection. So, he was offered as high priest

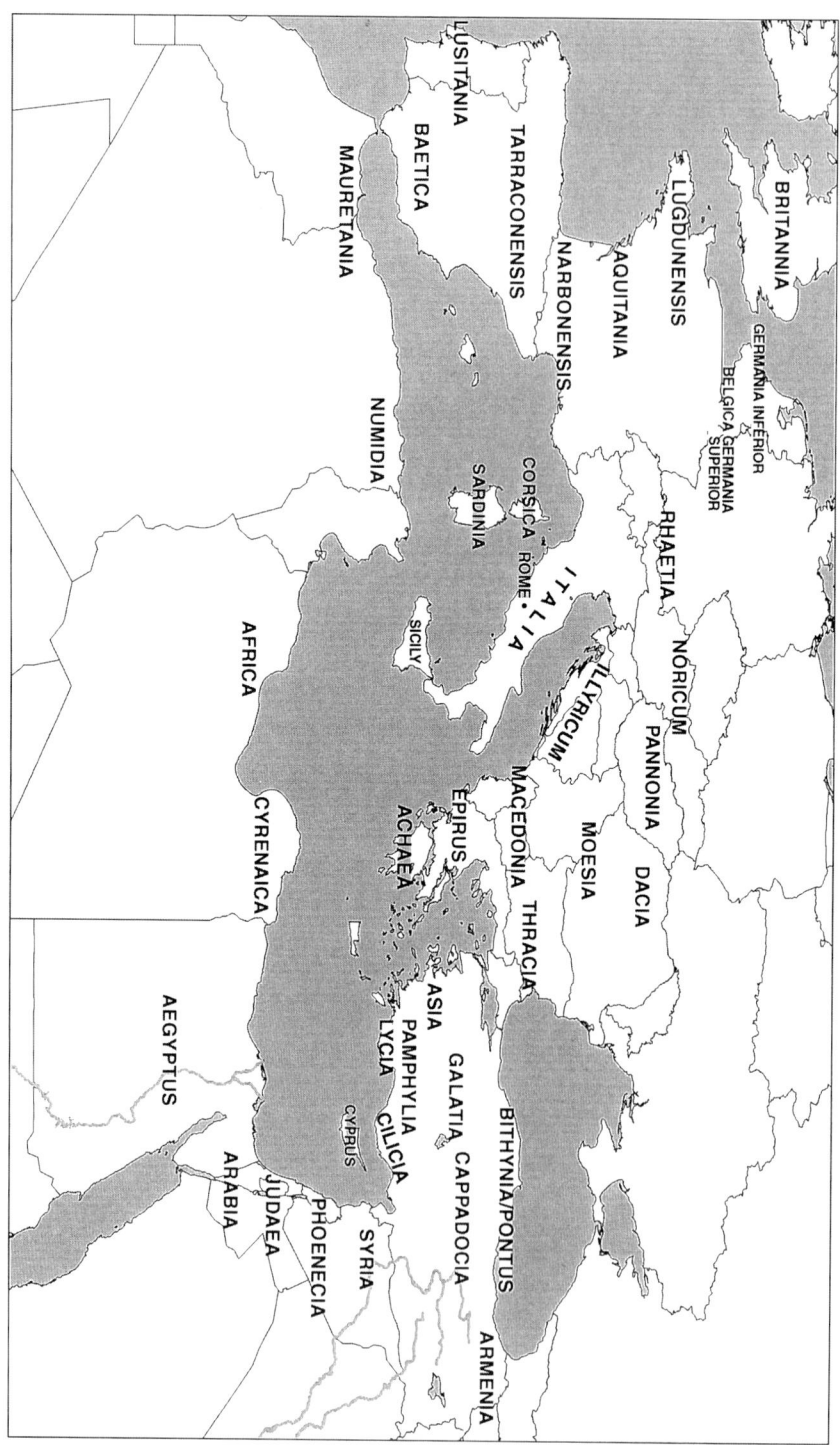

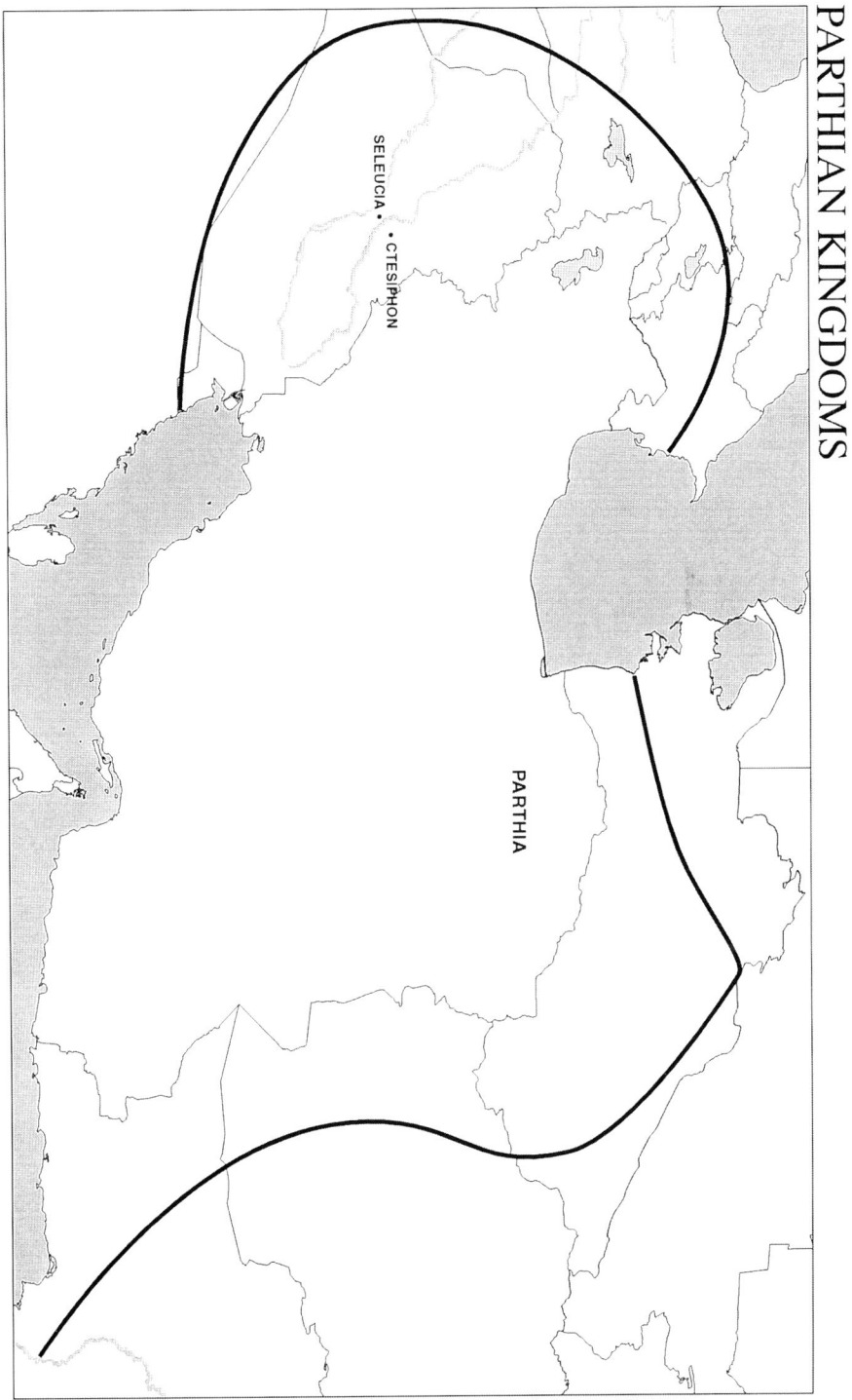

instead. The year, in all likelihood, was A.D. 33 [21]. Hindu sacred writings from the seventh century A.D. recount the journey a king had taken centuries earlier to the land of Palestine. Spotting a man sitting on a distant hill and wearing a white robe, he knew the man was a sage. In conversation, the Indian received instruction that men were to worship God "in righteousness, truth, and pure oneness of mind [22]."

As Christianity prevailed over paganism, Christians downsized the sprawling empire into its Latin and Greek-speaking divisions [23]. Possessed by the ages stands the wisdom of their policies [24].

In the East, the state chose to involve itself in ecclesiastical affairs. Eastern Orthodoxy has since had the tendency to accept domination by governments in the lands of its residence. Separation of church from state was commanded for Rome. Having thereby strengthened itself, the Roman Catholic Church possessed its independence into the Medieval Age. Groups and individuals who could not stomach these arrangements took off to deserts and mountains [25].

Germanic barbarians finally overwhelmed the Empire of the West [26]. The mysterious epic *Beowulf* was written in this era. The origins of the legends it memorializes remain unknown [27].

Twin cities, Seleucia and Ctesiphon, predominated in Mesopotamia as the city of Babylon fell into gradual decline.

It had been at the commencement of its Golden Age that Rome passed its first legislation regarding the troublesome Christian belief. Adherents were not to be actively sought out or hunted down, but officials retained authority to punish those who publicly practiced this outlawed faith.

The year was 39 A.D. when the fourteenth and last apostle tasted his first of many persecutions and had to run for his life out of the city of Damascus, Syria [28]. One thousand nine hundred twenty years later, Pope John XXIII announced the twenty-first council of the Roman Catholic Church, commonly known as the Second Vatican Council [29].

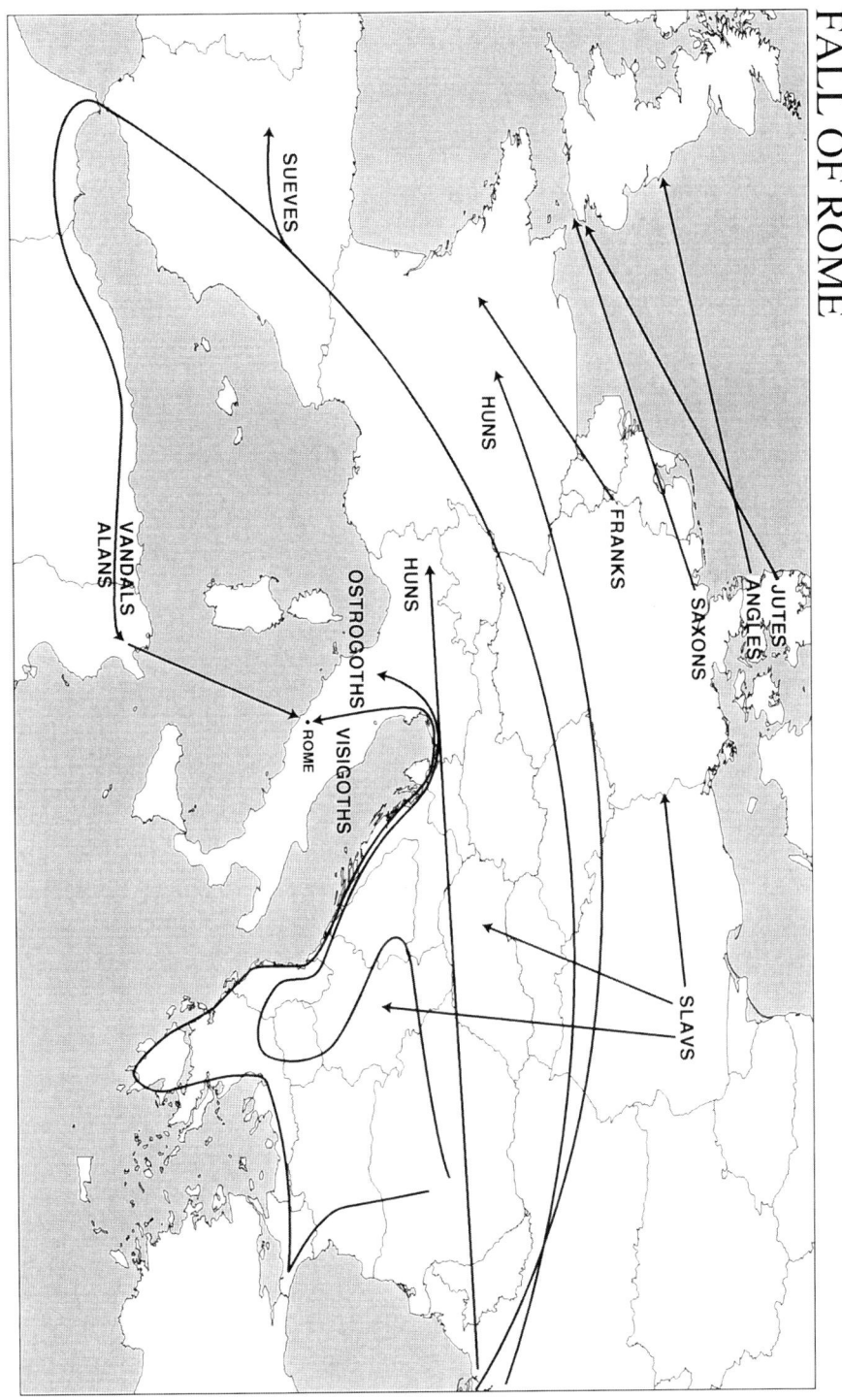

References

1. Exodus 20:2-6; Luke 3:9; Judges 13:1-16:31; Ruth; 1 Samuel 1:1-16:13

2. 1 Kings 11:1-12:24

3. 2 Kings 17:1-23

4. Matthew 1:2-16; Philippians 3:1-16; Acts 2:1-6:7

5. 2 Kings 22:1-25:30; Daniel 2:1-38

6. Jeremiah 25:12; Ezra 1:1-11; 7:1-28; Ezra

7. Nehemiah 2:1-6; Nehemiah

8. Ezekial 26:7; Jeremiah 4:6; 25:26

9. Daniel 11:7-20

10. Genesis 10:5, 18b

11. Daniel 2:39a; 5:1-31; 10:1-11:2

12. Daniel 11:4c

13. Daniel 2:39b; 11:3, 4ab

14. Jeremiah 51:7

15. Luke 2:1-3:2

16. Genesis 11:1-9; 10:25

17. Daniel 4:1-37; 8:1-8, 15-22

18. Daniel 7:1-8; 8:23a

19. 1 Samuel 8:1-22

20. Romans 1:18-32

21. 1 Thessalonians 5:1-11

22. Luke 4:16; Matthew 21:1-11; Mark 14:27-31; Mark 6:1-6

23. John 20:21,22

24. Matthew 13:1-52

25. John 20:23

26. Psalm 74; Psalm 91

27. Psalm 8; Exodus 14:19; 13:21; Psalm 2

28. Acts 9:1-30

29. Isaiah 2:2-4

CHAPTER THREE
MEDIEVAL AGES TO TWENTY-FIRST CENTURY

Muhammad made a fateful decision, in 622 A.D., to emigrate from Mecca to Medina because of opposition from wealthy Meccan traders touched off by his ideal of the *ummah,* or community of believers. The great prophet lived to see vindication when his faith and leadership were embraced by the Meccan establishment.

On the day of Muhammad's funeral, the faction from Mecca grasped authority. They moved swiftly, in the middle of a string of fierce battles, to unify Arabia, collect their late leader's sayings in a book called the Qur'an and direct military operations in the north. The accomplishments that grounded the religion of Islam were completed in 633 A.D., the year *after* the death of its visionary founder [1].

Parliamentary democracy is predominate throughout Europe today. It came about by means of a gradual evolution of institutions. What we might call "presidential democracy" was, in historical terms, created suddenly. It became quietly emulated by nations in South America and Africa [2].

References

1. Daniel 2:40; Revelation 2:26,27; 12:5; 19:15
2. Daniel 2:41-43; Luke 16:1-31

Chapter Four
The Number of the Antichrist

Three English language versions of the Bible translate it right. They are the Authorized (King James) Version of 1611, "Six hundred threescore *and* six;" the Revised Version of 1881–1885, "Six hundred and sixty and six;" and the American Standard Version of 1901, "Six hundred and sixty and six." The number was inscribed in the original texts by means of three Greek letters: Chi(X), or 600; Xi (E), or 60; and Stigma (C) or 6 [1]. "Counting" implies we should have focused more scrutiny on the directions before jumping to conclusions [2]. Mesopotamia's number system utilized a base of sixty. Egypt's was ten. Multiplied they set loose a *geometric progression* [3].

The prophecy of "Seventy Sevens" would appear to sanction a parallel line of inquiry [4]. The years 39, 93, and 633 stand *precisely* six, sixty, and six hundred years after the death and resurrection of Christ. Once revealed, these trails uncover the identities of building blocks, which, when deceitfully assembled, will unveil a global tyranny of character and proportion to be unsurpassed in the annals of human history [5].

I had assumed that the eastern religions and their "mystic" bent of mind were the bigger threat to faithfulness, but no, this is not so! With its comfortable lifestyle and a vast pantheon of gods and goddesses to absorb the loyalty and energies of its inhabitants, it was Egypt that was the more *spiritually* seductive for the people who loved God. Those directly involved or interested may elaborate on the influences of the Fertile Crescent *extending* to the kings of the North, but if you have not yet discerned a currently resurrected sequel of the king of the South, the biblical "place of refuge," the land *of the pharaohs,* you might ponder these *recent* popular performances: (1) the latest census statistics from great tracts of the United States of America, (2) the unexpected shifts in alignment of world power that took place as a Christian president, named Jimmy Carter, and a great man by the name of Muhammad Anwar el-Sadat, along with Menachem Begin of Israel, set in motion the Camp David Accords, and (3) the fact that eight signers of the Declaration of Independence and thirteen signers of the United States Constitution *were Masons.* And then take a look at a dollar bill [6].

And now, dear friend, with these final thoughts, we come to an understanding of a certain matter soon to be poured down upon us, to whit: when a deceiver of Islam cuts a deal with a betrayer of Christianity, then quickly gets in cahoots with a handful of bitter but well-placed Jews, we will see the emergence of the kingdom of the Antichrist, the final beast of Daniel's visions and of *Revelation's* chapters 13 and 17.

From the foggy reality of dream and spiritual visions, the prophet recovered to revive the aged 360 day calender [7], but his future looms in a literal and terrifying starkness should we provisionally envisage it labeled as *Judeo-Islamic-Christianity* [8].

She will settle on her self-appointed throne [9], only to realize she has been *displayed* [10] in the clutches of *Satanic guilt* [11]*!* Yet, red in any tone is a color that *stands out* [12].

A study of eschatology involves collating the passages. For those interested in such things, an appendix is supplied. In the Word of God, a name often denotes character, accomplishment, and position [13]. And, by the way, "six - six - six" is not an acceptable rendition [14].

References

1. Revelation 13:18b

2. Revelation 13:18a

3. Daniel 12:4

4. Daniel 9:1-27

5. Revelation 13:1-10

6. Daniel 11:5,6; Psalm 23

7. Daniel 9:24-27a; Revelation 11:2,3; 13:5; 12:6

8. 2 Timothy 3:1-17; Zechariah 5:5-11; Revelation 13:11-17

9. James 5:1-6

10. Matthew 24:32-25:46

11. 1 Timothy 6:10a

12. Revelation 17:1-18; Daniel 7:19-28; 8:9-14, 23-27; Matthew 7:6

13. Revelation 14:9-12; Daniel 2:44-49; 11:21-45

14. Revelation 19:19-20:6; 2 Corinthians 5:1-10; Revelation 20:7-15

CHAPTER FIVE
THE CANAANITE

The advanced power in its age, Jericho existed impregnable behind its massive stone wall —circa *8000 B.C.* [1], which would date its day of supremacy as having been millenniums prior to the moment a naive Adam and Eve acted to wager the chances of their developing nation to the east on a strategic alliance with its "god of fortresses [2]." They had neglected to honor an account of his intimidating gang of jaded adversaries, out from the mists of eternity past [3]. The city's name is derived from two Hebrew roots having to do with *timing:* the one is "fragrant," the other "moon [4]."

Their previous foreign exchange appears to have been in the direction of the Indus and Central Asia, where traces of revelation yet survive in pre-Indo-European mythology [5]. Figs could prove themselves to be crucial sustenance in the primitive Middle East. Their cultivation accounts for this plant's inclusion within the inspired body of allegory we have learned as *Genesis* to *Revelation* [6]. The leaves of the tree are the natural life. Its fruit is the spiritual life [7]. On the tree of life is found the righteous balance of fruit and leaves [8]. The tree of the knowledge of good and evil bears just leaves [9]. Jesus, too, had a word for this lifestyle: hypocrisy [10]. Fig trees had their place in the observances of pre-Aryan Hinduism. Legends out of India maintain that Adam and Eve once visited there.

"Also after that," Jericho's progeny continued, securing a nonconventional position in the table of nations while they collected around their tight-knit tribal communities— "And the Jebusite, and the Amorite, and the Girgashite; And the Hivite, and the Arkite, and the Sinite; And the Arvadite, and the Zemarite, and the Hamathite [11]." In other words, as Abraham and Sarah pursued their crusade to carry the Way into the land of Canaan, they were repeatedly amazed in finding out that somebody else had already brought it [12]. David retains his position as Old Covenant *type* of Christ the king, while the Holy Land's most important forerunner of Christ our high priest remains the *Canaanite* king, Melchizedek [13].

In Iranian mythology it is recorded that a council of twenty-four gods was convened prior to the completion of the rest of creation [14]. Their Maker made a move to do something, what I don't know, to put a buffer between Far Asia and India and fallen civilization [15]. *Salem* still means "peace." *Jeru* meant "to flow." Now it is set one Day to compute *Jerusalem* [16].

References

1. Joshua 6:26

2. Genesis 3:8-11; Daniel 11:38

3. Genesis 6:1-8

4. Deuteronomy 32:1-28; 1 Timothy 4:1-5; 2 Peter 2:1-22; Isaiah 40:27-31; Deuteronomy 32:29-43

5. Genesis 4:9-14a

6. Romans 3:1,2

    Acts 7:1-7

    Genesis 2:4; 5:1; 6:9; 10:1; 11:10; Exodus 17:14; Numbers 5:23; 21:14; Deuteronomy 28:58; Joshua 8:31; 10:13; 2 Samuel 1:18; Joshua 18:9; 1 Samuel 10:25; 1 Kings 11:41; 1 Chronicles 29:29; 2 Chronicles 12:15; 20:34; Ezra 4:15

    Isaiah 46:8-13

    Genesis 26:1-35

    Joshua 6:1-27

    Genesis 1:1

7. Matthew 21:18-22

8. Revelation 22:1-5

9. Genesis 3:7

10. Revelation 6:12-17

11. Genesis 6:4a; 10:16-18a; Numbers 13:22, 33; Deuteronomy 2:10-12, 20-23; 3:11

12. Acts 7:1-5; Genesis 12:1-20; 20:1-18

13. Psalm 110

14. Revelation 4:1-5:14

15. Genesis 3:24; Ezekiel 1:1-28; 10:1-22; Isaiah 6:1-13; Daniel 12:1-13

16. Genesis 10:1-32; 14:1-24; Zechariah 2:1-13; Daniel 7:9-28

THE MEANING OF THE NUMBERS OF THE ANTICHRIST

THE DOOMSDAY BOOK

Scripture	Other O.T.	Daniel 2	Daniel 7	Daniel 8	Daniel 9	Daniel 11	Matthew 24:4-31
Early Developments	Isaiah 14:20 Ezekial 28:16 Genesis 6:1-7 Danel 12:2,10 II Kings 6:16b	1-33,36-43	1-6, 17	1-8, 19-22		I-4 5-30	4-8
Firstfruits 3 1/2 years	Joshua 6:21 Exodus 24:6 "Half"			11	27a	31abc	9-12 13, 14a
Dividing Line	Daniel 12:3						14b
Approximate	Daniel 12:7			12	27b	31d	15, 21 29, 30
Harvest 3 1/2 years				13, 14		44, 45a	
Called and chosen with hearts of gold		34,35,44,45	27			"And the armies "And it was given	
Har-Magedon	Ezekiel 29:2-16; 39: 1-24 Daniel 12:12		11, 12, 18, 22c, 26	25c			

46

(or, Beware of Dogs)

Revelation 4:1-5:14; 12:6b	Revelation 6:1-17	Revelation 7:1-9:21 11:15-19	Revelation 10:1-11:14	Revelation 12:1-4, 6ac 13-17	Revelation 12:5, 7-12 13:1-18	Revelation 14:1-16:21	Revelation 17:1-18:24	Other N.T.
Third World discovers Christ	Seal 1 (1,2) Seals 2-4 (3-8)		Sweet when read, bitter when understood				17:1-12	I Tim 1:15 "arrangement, adornment" Luke 2:1 "inhabited earth" Heb. Ch. 9 Heb.12:26abc Rom. 3:23, 5:13b
	Seal 5 (9-11)			2 6ac	12:5	14:1	17:13,14	Gal. 4:26 Acts 7:53 Rev. 1:6b Luke 17:22-37; 21:8-28 Mk. 13:5-27 I Thess. 5:1-8
	Seal 6 (12-17)	7:3,4	11:2,3	13-17	12:7-12; 13:5	14:8 14:9-11	18:2	I Thess. 5:9-11
		7:14				15:2, 3a		I Thess. 4:15abc
		Seal 7 (8:1) 8:6 9:1-21				14:12		Heb. 12:26d Heb. 12:1a
		11:15				14:14-16		I Thess. 4:15d-18 I Cor. 15:51,52
		11:16-19 "which are in heaven followed him..." "unto her that she should array herself..."				15:5-16:21		Rev. 19:14a Luke 20:34-36 "age" Rev. 19:8a Luke 20:37, 38
						(16:12-16)		Rev. 19:17-21 II Thess. 2:8bc "epiphany of his presence"

Bibliography

Akeroyd, Richard H. *He Is Nigh*. Tuscaloosa: Portals Press, 1980.

Albright and Bugh. "Palestine." *The New Encyclopedia Britannica.* Fifteenth Edition. Macropaedia. Vol. 25. Chicago: Encyclopedia Britannica, Inc. 1997. pp. 409–11.

Ali, Dupree and Dupree. "Afghanistan." *The New Encyclopedia Britannica.* Fifteenth Edition. Macropaedia. Vol. 13. Chicago: Encyclopedia Britannica Inc., 1997. pp. 31–2.

Allchin, Frank Raymond. "India." *The New Encyclopedia Britannica.* Fifteenth Ediction. Macropaedia. Vol. 21. Chicago: Encyclopedia Britannica, Inc., 1997. pp. 26–36

Alter, Robert and Frank Kermode, eds. *The Literary Guide to the Bible*. Cambridge: Belknap Press, 1987.

Anderson, Sir Robert. *The Coming Prince*. Preface to the Tenth Edition. Grand Rapids: Kregel Classics, 1957. pp.viii–xvii.

Anderson, Sir Robert. *The Coming Prince.* Grand Rapids: Kregel Classics, 1957. pp.59–66.

Badian and Saller. "Ancient Greek and Roman Civilizations." *The New Encyclopedia Britannica.* Fifteenth Edition. Macropaedia. Vol. 20. Chicago: Encyclopedia Britannica, Inc., 1997. pp. 299–307

Baines, John R. "Egypt." *The New Encyclopedia Britannica*. Fifteenth Edition. Macropaedia. Vol. 18. Chicago: Encyclopedia Britannica, Inc. 1997 104–14

Baines, John R. "Middle Eastern Religions." *The New Encyclopedia Britannica.* Fifeenth Edition. Vol. 24. Chicago: Encyclopedia Britannica, Inc., 1997. pp. 106–111.

Baker, Hopwood and the Editors. "Egypt." *The New Encyclopedia Britannica.* Fifteenth Edition. Macropaedia. Vol. 18. Chicago: Encyclopedia Britannica, Inc., 1997. 141–2.

Barnard, Alan John. "Family and Kinship." *The New Encyclopedia Britannica.* Fifteenth Edition. Macropaedia. Vol 19. Chicago: Encyclopedia Britannica, Inc., 1997 pp. 72.

Barnes and The Editors. "Plato and Platonism." *The New Encyclopedia Britannica.* Fifteenth Edition. Macropaedia., Vol. 25. Chicago: Encyclopedia Britannica, Inc., 1997. pp. 893–4

Barnett, Ochsenwald and Bugh. "Lebanon." *The New Encyclopedia Britannica.* Fifteenth Edition. Macropaedia. Vol. 22. Chicago: Encyclopedia Britannica, Inc., 1007. pp. 894–6

Barraclough, Geoffrey, ed. *Harper Collins Atlas of World History.* Ann Arbor: Borders Press, 1999. pp. 60–1, 104–5.

Basham, van Buitenen and Doniger. "Hinuism." *The New Encyclopedia Britannica.*

Fifteenth Edition. Macropaedia. Vol. 20. Chicago: Encyclopedia Britannica, Inc., 1997. p. 522

Beeston, Alfred Felix L. "Arabia." *The New Encyclopedia Britannica.* Fifteenth Edition. Macropaedia. Vol. 13. Chicago: Encyclopedia Britannica, Inc., 1997. pp. 815–18.

Beitzel, Barry J. *The Moody Atlas of Bible Lands.* Chicago: Moody Press, 1985. p. 100.

Benario, Herbert W. tr. *Tacitus' Agricola, Germany and Dialogue on Orators.* Norman: University of Oklahoma Press, 1991. pp. 20–56.

Berry, George Ricker. *Interlinear Greek-English New Testament with a* Greek-English *Lexicon and New Testament Synonyms.* King James Version. Grand Rapids: Baker Book House, 1994. p. 649.

Boardman, Griffin and Murray, ed. *The Oxford History of the Roman World.* Introduction. Oxford: Oxford University Press, 1991. pp. 1–6.

Bokenkotter, Thomas. *A Concise History of the Catholic Church.* New York: Doubleday, 1990. p. 387.

Bowersock, G.W. *Greek Sophists in the Roman Empire.* London: Oxford University Press, 1969.

Bullinger, E.W. *Number in Scripture: Its Supernatural Design and Spiritual Significance.* Grand Rapids: Kregel Publications, 1967. p. 49.

Cary, Scullard and Saller, "Ancient Greek and Roman Civilizations." *The New Encyclopedia Britannica.* Fifteenth Edition. Macropaedia. Vol. 20. Chicago: Encyclopedia Britannica, Inc., 1997. pp. 287–90.

Childe, V. Gordon. *What Happened in History.* Hamondsworth, Middlesex: Penguin Books, Ltd., 1948. pp. 7–259.

Chilver, Guy Edward Farquhar. "Domitian." *The News Encyclpaedia Britannica.* Fifteenth Edition. Micropaedia. Vol. 4. Chicago: Enclycopaedia Britannica, Inc., 1997. pp. 168–9.

Clayton, Peter A. *Chronicle of the Pharaohs.* New York: Thames and Hudson, 1998. pp. 14–22, 27-29.

Collins, Robert O. "Sudan." *The New Encyclopedia Britannica.* Fifteenth Edition. Macropaedia. Vol. 28. Chicago: Encyclopedia Britannica, Inc., 1997. pp. 262–3.

Cowgill." *The New Encyclopedia Britannica.* Fifteenth Edition. Macropaedia. Vol. 22. Chicago: Encylcopaedia Britannica, Inc., 1997. pp. 582–4, 587–8.

Custance, Arthur C. M.A., Ph. D., F.R.A.I. *The Flood: Local or global? (Part II: Flood Taditions of the World), Doorway Papers No. 18.* Brookville, Ontario: Doorway Publications, 1989.

Custance, Arthur C. M.A., Ph. D., F.R.A.I. "Origin of the Nations: Genesis 10." *Doorway Papers.* Paper No. 5. Brockville, Ontario: Doorway Publications, 1988.

Dee, Jonathan. *Chronicles of Ancient Egypt.* London: Collins and Brown, 1998. pp. 32–63.

deGrummond, Nancy Thomson. "Ancient Greek and Roman Civilizations." *The New Encyclopedia Britannica.* Fifteenth Edition. Macropaedia. Vol. 20. Chicago: Encyclopedia Britannica, Inc. 1997. pp. 272–80.

Diakonoff, Igor Mikhailovich. "Languages of the World." *The New Encyclopedia Britannica.* Fifteenth Edition. Macropaedia. Vol. 22. Chicago: Encyclopedia Britannica, Inc., 1997. pp. 724–7.

Dowley, Tim, ed. *The Baker Atlas of Christian History.* Grand Rapids: Baker Books, 1997. p. 39.

Duruy, Victor. *History of Rome.* tr. by Ripley, M.M. ed. by Mahaffy, The Rev. J.P. Vol. V. Section One. Chs. LXXVIII, LXXIX. Boston: Estes And Lauriat, 1890. pp. 177–304.

Duruy, Victor. *History of Rome.* tr. by Ripley, M.M. ed. by Mahaffy, The Rev. J.P. Vol. VII. Section One. Ch. XCII. Boston: Estes And Lauriat, 1890. pp. 74–95.

Duruy, Victor. *History of Rome.* tr. by. Ripley, M.M. ed. by. Mahaffy, The Rev. J.P. Vol. VIII. Section One. Ch. CIX. Boston: Estes And Lauriat, 1890. pp. 273–333.

Edzard, Dietz O. "The History of Ancient Mesopotamia." *The New Encyclopedia Britannica.* Fifteenth Edition. Macropaedia. Vol. 23. Chicago: Encyclopedia Britannica, Inc., 1997. pp.860–76.

Encyclopedia Britannica, Inc. "Agricola, Gnaeus Julius." *The New Encyclopedia Britannica.* Fifteenth Edition. Macropaedia. Vol. 1. Chicago: Encyclopedia Britannica, Inc., 1997. p. 154.

Encyclopedia Britannica, Inc. "Bo Tree." *The New Encyclopedia Britannica.* Fifteenth Edition. Micropedia. Vol. 2. Chicago: Encyclopedia Britannica, Inc., 1997. p. 305.

Encyclopedia Britannica, Inc. "Camp David Accords." *The New Encyclopedia Britannica.* Fifteenth Edition. Micropedia. Vol. 2. Chicago: Enclyclopaedia Britannica, Inc., 1997. p. 772.

Encyclopedia Britannica, Inc. "Cornwall." *The New Encyclopedia Britannica.* Fifteenth Edition. Micropedia. Vol. 3. Chicago: Encyclopedia Britannica, Ind., 1997. pp. 641–2.

Encyclopedia Britannica, Inc. "cypress." *The New Encyclopedia Britannica.* Fifteenth Edition. Micropedia. Vol. 3. Chicago: Encyclopedia Britannica, Inc., 1997. p. 826.

Encyclopedia Britannica, Inc. "Eastern Orthodoxy." *The New Encyclopedia Britannica.* Fifteenth Edition. Micropedia. Vol. 4. Chicago: Encyclopedia Britannica, Inc. 1997. pp. 335–6.

Encyclopedia Britannica, Inc. "Ficus." *The New Encyclopedia Britannica.* Fifteenth Edition. Micropedia. Vol. 4. Chicago: Encyclopedia Britannica, Inc. 1997. p. 762.

Encyclopedia Britannica, Inc. "giant." *The New Encyclopedia Britannica.* Fifteenth Edition. Micropedia. Vol. 5. Chicago: Encyclopedia Britannica, Inc. 1997. pp. 246–7.

Encyclopedia Britannica, Inc. "Haruspices." *The New Encyclopedia Britannica.* Fifteenth Edition. Micropedia. Vol. 5. Chicago: Encyclopedia Britannica, Inc. 1997. p.731.

Encyclopedia Britannica, Inc. "Julia Domna." *The New Encyclopedia Britannica.* Fifteenth Edition. Micropedia. Vol. 6. Chicago: Enclyclopaedia Britannica, Inc., 1997. p. 645.

Encyclopedia Britannica, Inc. "Jutland." *The New Encyclopedia Britannica.* Fifteenth Edition. Micropedia. Vol. 6. Chicago: Encyclopedia Britannica, Inc., 1997. p.667.

Encyclopedia Britannica, Inc. "Khuzestan." *The New Encyclopedia Britannica.* Fifteenth Edition. Micropedia. Vol. 6. Chicago: Encyclopedia Britannica, Inc., 1997. p. 847.

Encyclopedia Britannica, Inc. "Levant." *The New Encyclopedia Britannica.* Fifteenth Edition. Micropedia. Vol 7. Chicago: Encyclopedia Britannica, Inc., 1997. p. 304.

Encyclopedia Britannica, Inc. "Nerva." *The New Encyclopedia Britannica.* Fifteenth Edition. Micropedia. Vol 8. Chicago: Encyclopedia Britannica, Inc., 1997. p. 608.

Enclyclopaedia Britannica, Inc. "Nimrod." *The New Encyclopedia Britannica.* Fifteenth Edition. Micropedia. Vol 8. Chicago: Enclyclopaedia Britannica, Inc., 1997. pp. 715–16.

Enclyclopaedia Britannica, Inc. "nome." *The New Encyclopedia Britannica.* Fifteenth Edition. Micropedia. Vol. 8. Chicago: Encyclopedia Britannica, Inc., 1997. p. 753.

Encyclopedia Britannica, Inc. "Parliament." *The New Encyclopedia Britannica.* Fifteenth Edition. Micropedia. Vol. 9. Chicago: Encyclopedia Britannica, Inc., 1997. pp. 161–2.

Encyclopedia Britannica, Inc. "Pliny the Younger." *The New Encyclopedia Britannica.* Fifteenth Edition. Micropedia. Vol 9. Chicago: Encyclopedia Britannica, Inc. 1997. p. 521.

Enclyclopaedia Britannica, Inc. "pontifex." *The New Encyclopedia Britannica.* Fifteenth Edition. Micropedia. Vol. 9. Chicago: Encyclopedia Britannica, Inc., 1997. p. 600.

Encyclopedia Britannica, Inc. "president." *The New Encyclopedia Britannica.* Fifteenth Edition. Micropedia. Vol. 9. Chicago: Encyclopedia Britannica, Inc. 1997. 683–4.

Encyclopedia Britannica, Inc. "Roman Catholicism." *The New Encyclopedia Britannica.* Fifteenth Edition. Micropedia. Vol 10. Chicago: Encyclopedia Britannica, Inc. 1997. pp. 149–50.

Encyclopedia Britannica, Inc. "shaman." *The New Encyclopedia Britannica.* Fifteenth Edition. Micropedia. Vol. 10. Chicago: Encyclopedia Britannica, Inc., 1997. pp. 692–3.

Encyclopedia Britannica, Inc. "Sophist." *The New Encyclopedia Britannica.* Fifteenth Edition. Micropedia. Vol. 11. Chicago: Encyclopedia Britannica, Inc., 1997. p. 17.

Encyclopedia Britannica, Inc. "Sumer." *The New Encyclopedia Britannica.* Fifteenth Edition. Micropedia. Vol. 11. Chicago: Encyclopedia Britannica, Inc., 1997. p. 384.

Encyclopedia Britannica, Inc. "Susa." *The New Encyclopedia Britannica.* Fifteenth Edition. Micropedia. Vol 11. Chicago: Encyclopedia Britannica, Inc., 1997. p. 416.

Encyclopedia Britannica, Inc. "Tartessus." *The New Encyclopedia Britannica* Fifteenth Edition. Micropedia. Vol. 11. Chicago: Enclyclopaedia Britannica, Inc. 1997. p. 568.

Encyclopedia Britannica, Inc. "Ten Lost Tribes of Israel." *The New Encyclopedia Britannica.* Fifteenth Edition. Micropedia. Vol. 11. Chicago: Encyclopedia Britannica, Inc., 1997. pp. 627–8.

Encyclopedia Britannica, Inc. "Vatican Council, Second." *The New Encyclopedia Britannica.* Fifteenth Edition. Micropedia. Vol 12. Chicago: Encyclopedia Britannica, Inc. 1997. p. 280.

Erman, Adolf. *Life in Ancient Egypt.* tr. by Tirard, H.M. Neew York: Dover Publications, Inc., 1971. pp. 1–28, 56, 259–72, 289–95, 307–8, 328–30, 351.

Ferfguson, John. "Ancient Greek, and Roman Civilizations." *The New Encyclopedia Britannica.* Fifteenth Edition. Micropedia. Vol. 20. Chicago: Encyclopedia Britannica, Inc., 1997. pp.264–7.

Forsythe, Gary Edward. "Ancient Greek and Roman Civilizations." *The New Encyclopedia Britannica.* Fifteenth Edition. Micropaedia. Vol. 20. Chicago:

Encyclopedia Britannica, Inc., 1997. pp. 280–7.

Fraser and Bugh. "Palestine." *The New Encyclopedia Britannica.* Fifteenth Edition. Micropedia. Vol. 25. Chicago: Encyclopedia Britinnica, Inc., 1997. pp. 411–15.

Frere, Sheppard Sunderland. "United Kingdom." *The New Encyclopedia Britannica.* Fifteenth Edition. Micropedia. Vol. 29. Chicago: Encyclopedia Britannica, Inc. 1997. p.23.

Fryde and The Editors. "The Study of History." *The New Encyclopedia Britannica.* Fifteenth Edition. Micropedia. Vol. 20. Chicago: Encyclopedia Britannica, Inc., 1997. pp. 559–62.

Frye, Richard N. "The History of Ancient Mesopotamia." *The New Encyclopedia \Britannica.* Fifteenth Edition. Micropedia. Vol. 23. Chicago: Encyclopedia Britannica, Inc., 1997. pp. 886–92.

Gadd and Ochsenwald. "Syria." *The New Encyclopedia Britannica.* Fifteenth Edition. Micropedia. Vol. 28. Chicago: Encyclopedia Britannica, Inc., 1997. pp. 367–8.

Ghul and Beeston. "Arabia." *The New Encyclopedia Britannica.* Fifteenth Edition. Micropedia. Vol. 13. Chicago: Encyclopedia Britannica, Inc., 1997. p. 815.

Gimbutas, Marija. "Prehistoric Peoples and Cutlures." *The New Encyclopedia Britannica.* Fifteenth Edition. Micropedia. Vol.26. Chicago: Encyclopedia Britannica, Inc., 1997. pp. 53–5.

Glubb, Sir John. *The Life and Times of Muhammad.* Chelsea: Scarbrough House/Publications, 1991. p. 129, 367.

Grant, Michael. "European Religions, Ancient." *The New Encyclopedia Britannica.* Fifteenth Edition. Micropedia. Vol. 18. Chicago: Encyclopedia Britannica, Inc., 1997. pp. 791–8.

Hambly, Gavin R.G. "Central Asia." *The New Encyclopedia Britannica.* Fifteenth Edition. Micropedia. Vol. 15. Chicago: Encyclopedia Britannica, Inc., 1997. pp. 705–7.

Hammond, Mason. "Trajan." *The New Encyclopedia Britannica.* Fifteenth Edition. Micropedia. Vol. 11. Chicago: Enclyclopaedia Britannica, Inc., 1997. pp. 890–1.

Harrison, Richard John. "Spain." *The New Encyclopedia Britnannica.* Fifteenth Edition. Micropedia. Vol. 28. Chicago: Encyclopedia Britannica, Inc., 1997. pp. 18–20.

Hislop, Rev. Alexander. *The Two Babylons.* Neptune: Loizeaux Brothers, 1959. p. 44, 247–8.

Hoehner, Harold W. *Chronological Aspects of the Life of Christ.* Grand Rapids: Academie Books, 1997. pp. 65–143.

Honko, Lauri O. "European Religions, Ancient." *The New Encyclopedia Britannica.* Fifteenth Edition. Micropedia. Vol. 18. Chicago: Encyclopedia Britannica, Inc., 1997. pp. 774–8.

Hood and Vermeule. "Ancient Greek and Roman Civilizations." *The New Encyclopedia Britannica.* Fifteenth Edition. Micropedia. Vol. 20. Chicago: Encyclopedia Britannica, Inc., 1997. pp. 205–18.

Hornblower, Simon. "Ancient Greek and Roman Civilizations." *The New Encyclopedia Britannica.* Fifteenth Edition. Micropedia. Vol. 20. Chicago: Encyclopedia Britannica, Inc., 1997. pp. 218–64.

Hunt and The Editors. "Cyprus." *The New Encyclopedia Britannica.* Fifteenth Edition.

Micropedia. Vol. 16. Chicago: Encyclopedia Britannica, Inc., 1997. pp. 898–9.

Irvine, Verity Elizabeth. "Jordan." *The New Encyclopedia Britannica.* Fifteenth Edition. Micropedia. Vol. 22. Chicago: Encyclopedia Britannica, Inc., 1997. p. 375.

Jacobsen, Thorkild. "Middle Eastern Religions." *The New Encyclopedia Britannica.* Fifteenth Edition. Micropedia. Vol. 24. Chicago: Encyclopedia Britannica, Inc., 1997. pp. 96–106.

Jones and Bugh. "Palestine." *The New Encyclopedia Britannica.* Fifteenth Edition. Micropedia. Vol. 25. Chicago: Encyclopedia Britannica, Inc., 1997. p. 415.

Kenyon and Bugh. "Palestine." *The New Encyclopedia Britannica.* Fifteenth Edition. Micropedia. Vol. 25. Chicago: Encyclopedia Britannica, Inc., 1997. pp. 408–9.

Kenyon and The Editors. "Jericho." *The New Encyclopedia Britannica.* Fifteenth Edition. Micropedia. Vol. 6. Chicago: Encyclopedia Britannica, Inc., 1997. 534–5.

Kitagawa, Tucci and Reynolds. "The Buddha and Buddhism." *The New Encyclopedia Britannica.* Fifteenth Edition. Micropedia. Vol. 15. Chicago: Encyclopedia Britannica, Inc., 1997. pp. 270–1.

Kovacs, Maureen Gallery, tr. *The Epic Of Gilgamesh.* Stanford: Stanford University Press, 1989.

Lang, G.H. *The Histories and Prophesies of Daniel.* Miami Springs: Conley & Schoettle Publishing Co., Inc., 1985.

Lloyd and Collon. "Turkey and Ancient Anatolia." *The New Encyclopedia Britannica.* Fifteenth Edition. Micropedia. Vol. 28. Chicago: Encyclopedia Britannica, Inc., 1997. pp. 932–6.

Lloyd and Easton. "Turkey and Ancient Anatolia." *The New Encyclopedia Britannica.* Fifteenth Edition. Micropedia. Vol. 28. Chicago: Encyclopedia Britannica, Inc., 1997. pp. 930–2.

Ochsenwald, William L. "Arabia." *The New Encyclopedia Britannica.* Fifteenth Edition. Micropedia. Vol. 13. Chcago: Encyclopedia Britannica, Inc., 1997. p. 808.

Olson, David R. "Writing." *The New Encyclopedia Britannica.* Fifteenth Edition. Micropedia. Vol. 29. Chicago: Encylcopaedia Britannica, Inc., 1997. pp. 1028–9.

Owen, Peter D. "Painting, the Art of." *The New Encyclopedia Britannica.* Fifteenth Edition. Micropedia. Vol. 25. Chicago: Encylcopaedia Britannica, Inc., 1997. pp. 320–1.

Perowne and Prawer. "Jerusalem." *The New Encyclopedia Britannica.* Fifteenth Edition. Micropedia. Vol. 22. Chicago: Encylcopaedia Britannica, Inc., 1997. pp. 328–35.

Petit and MacMullen. "Ancient Greek and Roman Civilizations." *The New Encyclopedia Britannica.* Fifteenth Edition. Micropedia. Vol. 20. Chicago: Encyclopedia Britannica, Inc., 1997. pp. 323–37.

Podhajsky and The Editors. "Horses and Horsemanship." *The New Encyclopedia Britannica.* Fifteenth Edition. Micropedia. Vol. 20. Chicago: Encyclopedia Britannica, Inc., 1997. p. 646.

Prakash, Acharya Daya. *Fulfillment of the Vedic Quest in the Lord Jesus Christ.* Lucknow, U.P.: Lucknow Publishing House, 1982. pp. 56–7.

Rahman and The Editors. "Muhammad and the Religion of Islam." *The New Encyclopedia Britannica.* Fifteenth Edition. Micropedia. Vol. 22. Chicago: Encyclopedia Britannica, Inc., 1997. pp. 8.

Rahula and Reynolds. "The Buddha and Buddhism." *The New Encyclopedia Britannica.* Fifteenth Edition. Micropedia. Vol. 15. Chicago: Encyclopedia Britannica, Inc., 1997. pp. 264–9.

Rebsamen, Frederick. *Beowulf: A Verse Translation.* New York: Haprer Collins Publsihers, 1991.

Rentz and Nijim. "Arabia." *The New Encyclopedia Britannica.* Fifteenth Edition. Micropedia. Vol. 13. Chicago: Encyclopedia Britannica, Inc., 1997. pp. 812–14.

Saggs, H.W.F. *People of the Past: Babylonians.* Berkeley: University of California Press, 2000. pp. 20-65.

Saller, Richard P. "Ancient Greek and Roman Civilizations." *The New Encyclopedia Britannica.* Fifteenth Edition. Micropedia. Vol. 20. Chicago: Encyclopedia Britannica, Inc., 1997. pp. 290–9. 307–8.

Salmon and MacMullen. "Ancient Greek and Roman Civlilizations." *The New Encyclopedia Britannica.* Fifteenth Edition. Micropedia. Vol. 20. Chicago: Encyclopedia Britannica, Inc., 1997. pp. 308–23.

Samuel and Bowman. "Egypt." *The New Encyclopedia Britannica.* Fifteenth Edition. Micropedia. Vol. 18. Chicago: Encyclopedia Britannica, Inc., 1997. pp. 123–6.

Schmidt and Ronan. "Calendar." *The New Encyclopedia Britannica.* Fifteenth Edition. Micropedia. Vol. 15. Chicago: Encyclopedia Britannica, Inc., 1997. pp. 420–1.

Schueler and Schueler. *Egyptian Magick.* St. Paul: Llewellyn Publications, 1997. pp. 62–68.

Smith and LeVeque. "Arithmetic." *The New Encyclopedia Britannica.* Fifteenth Edition. Micropedia. Vol. 14. Chicago: Encyclopedia Britannica, Inc., 1997. p. 76.

Smith, David Roger. "Central Asia." *The New Encyclopedia Britannica.* Fifteenth Edition. Micropedia. Vol. 15. Chicago: Encyclopedia Britannica, Inc., 1997. 701–4.

Smith, Wiliam, L.L.D. *Smith's Bible Dictionary.* ed. by Peloubet and Peloubet. Nashville: Thomas Nelson Publishers, 1986. pp. 72–3, 221,467, 622, 627.

Starr, Chester G. *A History of the Ancient World.* Fourth Edition. New York: Oxford Univrsity Press, 1991. pp 3-499.

Strohl, G. Ralph. "Jainism." *The New Encyclopedia Britannica.* Fifteenth Edition. Micropedia. Vol. 22. Chicago: Encyclopedia Britannica, Inc., 1997.pp. 247–9.

Strong, James. LL.D., S.T.D. *The New Strong's Exhaustive Concordance of the Bible.* Dictionary of the Hebrew Bible. Nashville: Thomas Nelson Publishers, 1990. pp. 19, 27, 37, 38, 52, 79, 81, 85, 94, 97, 107, 113, 117.

Strong, James LL.D., S.T.D. *The New Strong's Exhaustive Concordance of the Bible.* Main Concordance. Nashville: Thomas Nelson Publishers, 1990. pp. 101–2, 217, 304, 322, 396–7, 477, 497, 558–61, 632, 742, 784, 822, 907.

Summers,Montague. *The History of Witchcraft.* New York: Carol Publishers Group, 1993. pp. 175–6.

ten Cate, Philo H.J. Houwink. "Turkey and Ancient Anatolia." *The New Encyclopedia Britannica.* Fifteenth Edition. Mcropaedia. Vol. 28. Chicago: Encylcopaedia Britannica, Inc., 1997. pp. 936–41.

The Editors. "Iran." *The New Encyclopedia Britannica.* Fifteenth Edition. Micropedia. Vol. 21. Chicago: Encyclopedia Britannica, Inc., 1997. pp. 938–59.

Unger, Merrill F. *Unger's Bible Dictionary.* Chicago: Moody Press, 1966. p. 733, 832.

Unseen Journey: The Mystery, Myth and Truth of Freemasonry. Oak Brook: Eye Films and Video. 1991.

Vine, Unger and White, Jr. *Vine's Complete Expository Dictionary of Old and New Testament Words.* Nashville: Thomas Nelson Publishers, 1985. pp. 32, 79, 111, 685.

von Soden, Wolfram. *The Ancient Orient.* tr. by Schley, Donald G. Grand Rapids: William B. Eerdmans Publishing Company, 1993. pp. 1–41.

von Soden, Wolfram. "The History of Ancient Mesopotamia." *The New Encyclopedia Britannica.* Fifteenth Edition. Micropedia. Vol. 23. Chicago: Encyclopedia Britannica, Inc., 1997. pp. 876–86.

Walbank and The Editors. "Alexander the Great." *The New Encyclopedia Britannica.* Fifteenth Edition. Micropedia. Vol. 13. Chicago: Encylcopaedia Britannica, Inc., 1997. pp. 224–8.

Waldman, Marilyn R. "Islamic World." *The New Enclycopaedia Britannica.* Fifteenth Edition. Micropedia. Vol. 22. Chicago: Enclycopaedia Britannica, Inc., 1997. pp. 103–8.

Warmington, Brian H. "North Africa." *The New Enclycopaedia Britannica.* Fifteenth Edition. Micropedia. Vol. 24. Chicago: Enclycopaedia Britannica, Inc., 1997. pp. 949–54.

Watt and The Editors. "Muhammad and the Religion of Islam." *The New Encyclopedia Britannica.* Fifteenth Edition. Micropedia. Vol. 22. Chicago: Enclycopaedia Britannica, Inc., 199. pp. 1–5.

Welch, Kathryn. *The Romans.* New York: Rizzoli International Publications, Inc., 1998. pp. 8–35.

Wente and Baines. "Egypt." *The New Encyclopedia Britannica.* Fifteenth Edition. Micropedia. Vol. 18. Chicago: Encyclopedia Britannica, Inc., 1997. pp. 114–23.

Whiston, William, tr. *The New Complete Works of Josephus.* Against Apion. Book 1. Section 14. Grand Rapids: Kregel Publications, 1999. pp. 941–2.

Widengren, Geo. "Iranian Religions." *The New Encylcopedia Britannica.* Fifteenth Edition. Micropedia. Vol. 9. Chicago: Encyclopedia Britannica, Inc., 1983. p. 870.

Wolters, Oliver W. "Indonesia." *The New Encyclopedia Britannica.* Fifteenth Edition. Micropedia. Vol. 21. Chicago: Encyclopedia Britannica, Inc., 1997. pp. 235–6.

www.census.gov